PRAISE FOR 'THE CRUELTY OF FREE WILL'

Alphabetically:

"Oerton has done it again: a delightful, wise and compassionate diagnosis of the free will error, and why correcting it matters so much."

– Tom Clark, *Director of the Center for Naturalism, USA*

"*The Cruelty of Free Will* contains an unpretentious and heart-felt denial of the sort of free will that supports retribution, whether championed by compatibilists, libertarians or illusionists. Oerton's denial of free will places itself squarely in the determinist, materialist and atheist traditions. His denunciation of moral responsibility is so straightforward yet profound that even those who are most strongly committed to this idea may feel impelled to rethink their attachment. Highly recommended for anyone who has ever been tempted to assign 'just deserts' – that is, for everyone."

– Richard Double, *Emeritus Professor of Philosophy, University of Pennsylvania*

"On a large subject about which there is common belief, good sense is rare. So is amiable lucidity. And humanity. This book has them."

– Ted Honderich, *Grote Professor Emeritus of the Philosophy of Mind and Logic, University College London*

"Moral responsibility and just deserts promote human dignity, protection of the innocent, equal opportunity, and respect for individual rights: or so both philosophers and "the folk" generally believe. That deep conviction makes it essential to preserve belief in moral responsibility at all costs. Richard Oerton demolishes that belief with wit, insight, and clarity, and this demolition work clears the ground for building a more humane and decent and scientifically sound system."

– Bruce Waller, *Professor of Philosophy, Youngstown State University*

PRAISE FOR 'THE NONSENSE OF FREE WILL'

Endorsements

"Most people are completely taken in by the illusion of free will. Happily, Richard Oerton is not among them. *The Nonsense of Free Will* is a wonderfully clear – and very clever – little book."

> – Sam Harris, *author of the New York Times bestsellers* The End of Faith, Letter to a Christian Nation, The Moral Landscape *and* Free Will

"There are philosophical, scientific, novel, determined, American, pompous, dotty and other books on free will and determinism. There are also a few books that are lucid and informal introductions for ordinary readers and let you know that your free will does not exist. Richard Oerton's may be the best of these."

> – *Ted Honderich, Grote Professor Emeritus of the Philosophy of Mind and Logic, University College London*

"This book is superbly written and a delight to read. Starting as a clearly reasoned treatment of determinism, it merges seamlessly into a critique of English criminal law and penal policy, and ends with a plea for society to abandon what the author sees as its irrational belief in free will."

> – *Joshua Rozenberg, Q.C., lawyer and legal commentator, formerly legal editor of* The Daily Telegraph

"This fascinating book explains and discusses one of the most difficult questions underlying criminal liability – are we right to work on the basis that all sane people can exercise 'free will'? Richard Oerton explores the free will v. determinism debate with remarkable and rare clarity. This is not a book only for academics: it is of vital interest to all who want to think about the way society is organised."

> – *Stephen Cretney, D.C.L., F.B.A., Q.C., LL.D., Emeritus Fellow of All Souls College, Oxford*

Reviews

"This is a terrific book … so clear and readable that it would be appropriate for general readers, introductory philosophy courses, and undergraduate courses in criminal justice and the humanities."

— *Richard Double, Emeritus Professor of Philosophy, University of Pennsylvania*

"[W]hat I loved about your book [is that you] have an unsurpassed grasp of the deep issues in free will and reach the most reasonable conclusions, without becoming sidetracked by the philosophical jargon that impedes professional philosophers."

— *Professor Double, in a personal communication to the author*

"I have read a fair amount about this subject. Much of it has been excellent. But nothing I ever read got to the core of things the way Oerton does. No one ever made their case with such a combination of simplicity and surgical precision. Free will is a vast issue. Vast and slippery and mysterious. To tackle it is no small undertaking. Oerton, however, makes it easy. He demystifies free will."

— *Stephen Campana*

"Oerton has written a terrific book, a must read for anyone interested in the free will debate and why it matters. He reaches all the right conclusions, for the right reasons, stated most felicitously … a delightful read — unassuming, straightforward, informed and funny."

— *Tom Clark, Director of the Center for Naturalism, USA*

For the full review see:
www.naturalism.org/resources/book-reviews/the-rise-of-the-new-determinists

"What Richard Dawkins did for atheism, Richard Oerton has here done for determinism. *[Author's note: Though grateful for this comment, I think it might be a very slight exaggeration.]* [H]e has taken all those doubts about the existence of free will … and distilled them into an intelligent, accessible and highly engaging polemic. I would urge anyone with any doubts about free will to read this book; to read one's own inchoate ideas expressed in such a clear and concise matter is simply exhilarating … *The Nonsense of Free Will* has provided the encouragement I needed to finally accept determinism and its implications, and I suspect that there will be many others for whom this book will have a similar effect."

— *Benjamin Langlois on* LibraryThing

"Every summer I try to introduce undergraduates who are thinking about choosing the criminology, sentencing and penal system course to some "holiday" reading that will get them thinking ... Had I read this book in time, it would definitely have been on the list. It will be there next year. This is a thoughtful and thought-provoking book."

– Loraine Gelsthorpe, *Professor in Criminology and Criminal Justice, Institute of Criminology, University of Cambridge*

Other comments on Amazon

"I ... was truly taken aback by the clarity and simplicity with which Oerton approaches this cloudy subject ... a fantastic writer and a straight communicator"

"... a brilliant achievement and a triumphant piece of scholarly writing"

"A very clear and fair account of the problems associated with the concept of free will. Whatever your views are before reading you will be much better informed after finishing this book"

"... shows that no great intellect is needed to dispel free will ... most people will gain a tremendous amount of insight from reading this book"

"If you are looking for an easy to read yet powerful explanation of the determinism v. free will contest then I strongly recommend this book"

"... presents clear, precise arguments that are well structured and persuasive ... should leave you wondering why you believed in free will in the first place and with a whole new perspective on life"

"I absolutely loved [this] book"

"An easy to read and understand, fun and well written argument for the nonsense of free will"

" ... a fantastic addition to the growing literature about how we interpret a world without free will ... Since it is free of excessive philosophy jargon the text is very accessible for those new to the topic and still rich and rewarding for those more familiar. A 'must read' ..."

"Highly recommended"

"Wonderfully written and – to my mind – totally persuasive"

"Nice perspective from someone familiar with the legal system ... honest, refreshingly human and full of good sense"

"This is one of the best, balanced and fair books which show 'free will' for what it really is, a nonsense idea. Nonsense, in that it can't even be mapped on to reality"

"Brilliantly explained"

"Thought the book was nonsense!"

[Author's note: Astonishingly, there are a few other unfavourable reviews available to anyone who cares to look for them.]

THE
CRUELTY
OF
FREE WILL

HOW SOPHISTRY AND SAVAGERY
SUPPORT A FALSE BELIEF

RICHARD OERTON

Author of
THE NONSENSE OF FREE WILL
Facing up to a false belief

Copyright © 2016 Richard Oerton

The moral right of the author has been asserted.

Apart from any fair dealing for the purposes of research or private study, or criticism or review, as permitted under the Copyright, Designs and Patents Act 1988, this publication may only be reproduced, stored or transmitted, in any form or by any means, with the prior permission in writing of the publishers, or in the case of reprographic reproduction in accordance with the terms of licences issued by the Copyright Licensing Agency. Enquiries concerning reproduction outside those terms should be sent to the publishers.

This is a work of fiction. Names, characters, businesses, places, events and incidents are either the products of the author's imagination or used in a fictitious manner. Any resemblance to actual persons, living or dead, or actual events is purely coincidental.

Matador
9 Priory Business Park,
Wistow Road, Kibworth Beauchamp,
Leicestershire. LE8 0RX
Tel: 0116 279 2299
Email: books@troubador.co.uk
Web: www.troubador.co.uk/matador
Twitter: @matadorbooks

ISBN 978 1785899 928

British Library Cataloguing in Publication Data.
A catalogue record for this book is available from the British Library.

Printed and bound in the UK by TJ International, Padstow, Cornwall
Typeset in 11pt Bembo by Troubador Publishing Ltd, Leicester, UK

Matador is an imprint of Troubador Publishing Ltd

This book is dedicated

with love
to all the living members of my family and
to the memory of those who have died

and

to all those who see free will for
the nonsense it is,
feel none the worse,
and get on with their lives

Acknowledgements

I am very grateful to James Miles, author of *The Delusion of Free Will: How we Settled for the Illusion of Morality,* for reading this book in draft, for pointing out several errors and for making some very useful suggestions; but the finished version is no fault of his.

I want to thank also those who have been kind enough to endorse the book, all of whom must have had much better things to do with their time than to wade through it.

"The worst of all cruel creeds and of all bloody wrongs inflicted by the past can be found in the barbarous belief that man is a free moral agent."

Clarence Darrow, American trial lawyer,
speaking at Easter 1888 [1]

"And so, to the end of history, murder shall breed murder, always in the name of right and honour and peace, until the Gods are tired of blood and create a race that can understand."

George Bernard Shaw, *Caesar and Cleopatra (Act IV)*

"Men fear thought as they fear nothing else on earth … Thought is subversive and revolutionary, destructive and terrible, thought is merciless to privilege, established institutions and comfortable habits; thought is anarchic and lawless, indifferent to authority, careless of the well-tried wisdom of the ages … Thought is … the light of the world, and the chief glory of man."

Bertrand Russell, *Why Men Fight* [2]

Contents

Preface   xiii

1. Tell me the old, old story   1
A recapitulation

2. Looking into the abyss   8
Reason and unreason in free will philosophy

3. Accept no substitutes   14
Free will philosophy and sleight of hand

4. What's in a name?   26
The disputed meanings of "free will"

5. A short trip to Frankfurt   30
An example of philosophical sophistry

6. Free will and hypocrisy   33
How we accept determinism in all but name

7. If you're not rich, blame yourself   39
The cruelty of free will belief

8. Moral responsibility and Martin Luther   47
The faulty foundations of retribution

9. Vengeance is ours   57
The interdependence of free will and human savagery

10. They're made to do it over and over   69
But let's kill them anyway

11. Serves that piece of crap right   72
A penal policy without retribution

12. A new heart also will I give you, and a new spirit put within you   88
Re-making the criminal

13. *Pas devant les enfants*   95
Determinism as a dirty secret

14. I'm invited to the investiture   102
But I don't think I'll go

15. Was it for this the clay grew tall?   106
Happy 200,000[th] birthday, *homo sapiens*

Appendix: a summary   113

Notes   117

Preface

Free will really is a dead duck. By "free will" I mean the free will in which most people believe: the idea that we might make choices different from the ones we do make – the idea that, despite being exactly the same people in the exactly the same situations, we really might behave on any given occasion in any one of two or more different ways. This mustn't be confused with the idea that we *could* behave differently: of course we could, if we wished, behave in any of the ways that our physical capacity would allow. My own physical capacity is diminishing with old age but I can still do a lot of different things. That's not the point. The point is that, like everyone else, I am built by my biological inheritance and past experiences to have the character, the nature, the brain that I have, and it is inconceivable that I might act independently of these things. I behave as I do because I am the person I am: my behaviour is determined by my being that person. If it were not, then surely I should not be me but some strange and unpredictable entity whom no one would recognise and no one could understand; and I should be unknown even to myself.

Determinism is not an abstract intellectual theory, but a rather obvious aspect of our existence. I don't see how anyone who has really thought – thought objectively and thought hard – about the human condition can have ended up by believing that we have the kind of free will I have described. I tried to give my own reasons for disbelief in a book called *The Nonsense of Free Will* [1] (to which I shall refer from here onwards as *NFW*). I give a brief recapitulation of those reasons in Chapter 1 of this book, but after that I shall take the absence of this free will pretty much for granted and concentrate instead on two related questions: bearing in mind that its absence really is as plain as a pikestaff to many philosophers and neuroscientists and to other people like me, and that our disbelief is based on largely undisputed facts, *why* ... and *how* ... does free will belief persist so stubbornly both among the general public and among some philosophers? This is a book about what makes us want to keep free will in place, and how we try to do it. I touched on these questions in the earlier book – and little quotes from it adorn most of the chapter headings of this one – but I believe there's more to be said about them.

The tenacity of free will belief does call for an explanation. I think the explanation is to be found in most people's strong desire to preserve and justify what I might call the existing dispensation – the social and moral status quo [2]. And I think that what underlies this desire is a human characteristic that I have to call savagery. This desire and this characteristic are a part of our natures, so they come naturally to us, and the idea of free will seems to validate and justify what comes naturally. In later chapters I hope to explain what I mean by this, and to draw attention to the harm that continues to flow from belief in free will. Disbelievers, it seems to me, have not only logic, rationality and common sense on their side, but right, justice and morality as well. Free will belief is not a good thing but a bad thing, and its results are not desirable but shameful. The persistent belief that human beings can exercise free choice goes far to destroy sympathy for those whose lives are bleak (because they are thought to have only themselves to blame for failing to improve their situations) and to encourage retributive and vengeful attitudes towards those who do harm (because they are thought to have created their own wickedness). Philosophers and others who set out to uphold free will, or to offer us some different and amorphous version of it, seem often to think that they are doing us a favour.

Sadly, many of us agree and are duly grateful. Ultimately, in my view, this gratitude is wholly misplaced.

It may be that, at this stage in the story of human evolution, our continuing savagery will stand in the way of any general and explicit acceptance of determinism and its consequences. But attitudes can change; we who reject free will may play some small part in changing them; and we can make the attempt with enthusiasm and without apology.

1

Tell me the old, old story

A recapitulation

Our belief in free will is a false belief,
and we are better off without false beliefs
because any false belief enslaves us
even if it goes by a name which has
the word "free" in it. (NFW, p. xii)

There are still some people in the world – not quite as many as I feared there would be, but rather more than I could wish – who haven't read my earlier book, *The Nonsense of Free Will* (to which I'm referring as *NFW*). To those thus deprived, and to those who have read it but have understandably allowed its details to fade from their memories, I offer this brief recapitulation.

The case against free will – the free will which most people believe in: the free will which purports to embody free choice – can be stated very simply. We act as we do because we are the people we are, and we have not made ourselves the people we are. Let me expand on this a little:

1. Our inborn characteristics (our genetic inheritances, our biologies) are the product of the genes of two other people, possibly with a bit of random mutation thrown in.

The Cruelty of Free Will

2. These characteristics then develop as we grow up, interacting with the environment in which we find ourselves and which includes our parents or other people who have charge of us, our peers, our teachers, our living conditions and all the multitude of influences which affect us.

3. At any given moment in our lives, we are the products of this process – of these factors which have gone into making us the people we are. We behave as we do because we *are* the people we are and it is our behaviour which shows us to *be* the people we are.

In Victorian times lawyers invented a character called the reasonable man: he's the ordinary citizen, "the man on the Clapham omnibus". If I found myself sitting in a seat beside him and conveyed to him the gist of what I've just said, his reaction might well be to say, "Thank you for that staggering glimpse of the bleeding obvious. Don't waste any more of my time." But what might he say if I were then to suggest that he had just rejected free will and endorsed determinism? "Oh, well, in that case there must be something *wrong* with what you say. I'll tell my philosopher friends about this and they'll all write contradictory books about it and the whole subject will descend into such esoteric confusion that no one else will need to think about it ever again." And that is very much what seems to have happened. Some ideas about why it has happened appear later in this book.

Free will has always had a good press, and determinism a bad one. Determinism seems to embody an idea which we reject almost instinctively, whereas free will, like religion in times gone by, is accepted without question not just as a good thing but perhaps as something essential to the human condition. I believe we've got this exactly the wrong way round. To me, determinism is a natural and comforting thing and free will is an incoherent and disturbing one – almost a glimpse of insanity.

All that determinism means, of course, is that there are chains of causality, chains of cause and effect, beginning before our births, running on to make us the people we are, and running on into the ways in which we behave. Determinism isn't Fate. It isn't some inexorable force which exercises a kind of compulsion over us. It acts through our wishes and desires, not against them. We have choices to make and it is we alone who make them, but we make them in the way we do because we are the people we are – and we are the people we are because of the causal factors which have made us that way. Our choices give expression to the characters, the motivations, which our inborn natures and our past lives have given us. There is nothing alarming about this. Wouldn't it be very alarming indeed if it were not so?

But if we are to believe in free will we must believe that it is not so – that although we may be motivated wholeheartedly to do a particular thing, we may nonetheless turn aside and do something else. However strong were Adolf Hitler's motives to start the Second World War, he might nonetheless have opted for peace in his time. However strongly Nelson Mandela was motivated to act in such a way as to earn a Nobel Peace Prize, he might nonetheless, while remaining the same person in the same situation, have decided instead to plunge South Africa into civil war.

Really? Well, of course not. But this, whether or not we consciously acknowledge it, is what belief in free will entails. Of course Hitler was a hateful person and Mandela a lovable one and that's reason enough for us to hate the one and love the other, but our different feelings about them rest also, don't they, on the belief that it wasn't inevitable that they should have acted as they did, and that they really might not have done so? This is the idea of free will which we harbour if we profess to believe in it, and this is the idea of free will on which our criminal justice system rests.

In *NFW*, I have a character called Burglar Bill. He's a habitual burglar with a drug habit to pay for and he's standing at night in a deserted street outside an apparently empty house which looks likely

The Cruelty of Free Will

to contain a lot of good loot. His upbringing has left him with little in the way of a normal conscience. He has run out of money. He has a strong desire to break into the house, he has no qualms about doing so, and he doesn't expect to get caught. So he breaks in. No surprises there. But our criminal justice system – and our everyday conception of free will – require us to believe that he really *might*, he might *really*, have turned away and gone home to bed, and refrained from all crime in the future, despite having no motivation to do so.

Of course Burglar Bill was physically capable of turning away, and in that sense he could have done so – and he would have done so if he had wanted to. But he didn't want to. What is he supposed to do? There's no way he can claw out of thin air some moral scruple which he simply doesn't have, and why would he try? If he really had gone home to bed and refrained from further crime, he would have acted against his own wishes. It would have been even more of a surprise to him than to anyone else. And this is one of the places where the idea of free will falls apart because free will necessarily negates and destroys the connection between motivation and behaviour. Free will requires that we should be free from *ourselves*. If the possession of something called free will really does mean that we can act against the preponderance of our own motivations and may actually do so, then it becomes impossible to find causes for our behaviour. The price you have to pay for believing in free will is that you can never know why anyone does anything.

A great deal of effort, by those much better qualified than me, has gone into understanding the causes of crime. And probably most of us remember Tony Blair promising to be tough on crime and tough on its causes. To a determinist, all this makes sense; but if we really believe in free will then surely it doesn't, because for a believer in free will there can be only one cause of crime – namely, the criminal's wilful failure to refrain from committing it. Proponents of free will refuse to look beyond this or, if they do look, discount the importance of what they see. In 2010 Raoul Moat killed one person and very seriously injured two others before killing himself. Some sympathy was expressed, not only for his victims but for him. The Prime Minister, David Cameron, would have none of it. He told the House of Commons: "It is absolutely clear that Raoul Moat was a callous murderer, full stop, end of story." This is revealing. For those who believe in free will, as presumably Cameron does, a statement like this *has* to be the end of the story. There really has to be a full *stop* – a point at which you must stop thinking, close your mind and look no further. If Cameron's description of Moat is "end of story", there must be a story for it to be the end of, a story about what made Moat a callous murderer, a story at which Cameron does not want us to look.

Free will entails unpredictability. If a human act is an exercise of what we call free will, then it is by definition unpredictable even in principle. But no one really believes that this is so. Criminology could not exist if it were so. Nor could any science which concerns itself with human behaviour. In reality the advance of science makes behaviour increasingly predictable, not just in principle but to some extent in practice. Adrian Raine's book *The Anatomy of Violence* [1] shows that violent crime results from detectable brain abnormalities, and other research suggests that chemical imbalances play a part and that violence may result from faulty genetic endowment, particularly if combined with destructive upbringing. Now, apparently, there is even software which can be used to predict future re-offending.

This may be the moment at which some people would back away from a belief in complete free will but cling tenaciously to a watered down version of it – some idea that, although causality may have predisposed criminals to crime, there must nonetheless be a little bit of free will in there somewhere. But how would this work? Surely the idea of partial or downsized free will is still less coherent than the idea of free will itself. If we are to picture this modified version of free will as leaving us, not with an open playing field, but only with a small amount of wriggle room, then any particular crime may or may not have been within the wriggle room enjoyed by the particular criminal. If it was outside his wriggle room, then it can't have been a product of free will. But if it was within his wriggle room, then the same logical contradictions arise as in the case of simple free will. Why did he wriggle in the direction of doing it, rather than in the direction of not doing it? If there is an explanation for this, it must be a causal explanation, and this again would rule out free will. If there is no causal explanation, then we are left once again with a random, free-floating act which is simply unconnected to the criminal's nature.

And even if the idea of a little bit of free will were a coherent one, it would still get us nowhere because we should never know to what extent, if any, a particular act resulted from that little bit. The trouble with those who put forward this idea is that all too often they behave from then onwards (rather unscrupulously) as if they had vindicated the whole idea of free will and re-established a full and potent version of it – as if, in other words, their little bit amounted to the whole lot.

In *NFW* I suggested that acceptance of determinism might make a real difference to our attitudes to crime and penal policy, and that's why I've concentrated in the last few paragraphs on behaviour which is criminal. But what I've tried to say applies every bit as much to behaviour which is bad in other ways, to behaviour which is good in any possible way, and to behaviour which is neither good nor bad but just ordinary – in other words, to all human motivation.

Let me try to sum up at this point. Surely our whole conception of free will, reflected both in our everyday lives and in the justice system, is an attempt to have our cake and eat it. We demand that an act of free will must both reflect our character, our nature – show us for the people we are – and yet at the same time allow us to divorce ourselves from that character or nature and rise above it (or fall below it), doing so for no ascertainable reason. This "free will" in which so many people have so firm a faith, is not just a thing which doesn't exist: it's a thing which couldn't exist, a thing like a circle which is also square. There is nothing in the world – nothing you could imagine – which would fit our conception of free will.

For some people the case against free will is made, or strengthened, by the findings of neuroscience – and particularly by the experiments of Benjamin Libet and others, which appeared to show that our decisions do not originate in consciousness but are made by our unconscious brains before our conscious minds get to know about them. These findings caused the experimenters some consternation. They thought that, if the results had come out the other way round – so that decisions were shown to originate in the conscious mind, as they had supposed – then this would have vindicated free will, whereas what they actually did was to knock it on the head. These findings may convince you of determinism, but I see them as a bit of a sideshow. The idea that consciousness is to be equated with free will, or somehow embodies it, was surely never plausible in the first place. Our idea of free will remains an impossibility, still every bit as much of a square circle, wherever our decisions originate.

As I work my way towards the end of this chapter, I see an article in *The Times* [2] about computers, with a headline that reads: "Mankind must rise to the challenge of facing machines capable of wit, charm and resourcefulness". I myself lay little claim to wit, and even less to charm and resourcefulness, but plenty of people do display these characteristics to the full and we admire them for it. So we should. But there is a clear analogy here: just as these qualities are programmed into a computer, so they are programmed into the human brain [3]. The only difference is that in our case this is done, not by a programmer, but by a causal process. The end result is the same.

2

Looking into the abyss

Reason and unreason in free will philosophy

> [E]motional resistance to the idea of
> determinism is a far more potent obstacle
> in the way of its acceptance than any of
> the intellectual difficulties which people
> may think they have with it. (NFW, p. 85)

If I were younger and rather more intelligent and had a great deal of time on my hands, I might try to look at the way in which philosophy is skewed by emotional factors – to see, in fact, whether the emotion could be taken out of philosophy, or at least out of the philosophy of free will. I don't suggest, of course, that human emotion itself is not a fit subject for objective study by philosophers, though it may be a very tricky one. What I do suggest is that the content of their own philosophy often depends upon their own subjective, and probably unacknowledged, emotional approach to the subject – and that this is particularly true when the subject is free will.

In the ordinary way we don't distinguish between reason and emotion: we may even go through life without noticing that there is a distinction. But of course there is, and it's important in several different ways. The idea that 1+1=2 has no emotional content: it's a purely rational idea. But, as I pointed out in *NFW*[1], the attempt by

Bertrand Russell and A.N. Whitehead to prove logically that 1+1=2, which took them 350 pages of their *Principia Mathematica* and which was in itself (I imagine) an exercise in pure rationality, was fuelled, not by reason, but by a wish, an urge, a desire to do it. If we ourselves use a rational and emotionless mathematical calculation to serve some particular end, like working out the cost of four hot cross buns, the end must necessarily be one we want to achieve. And when we sit down to plan the best route to take us from one place to another we are making use of rationality alone, but we shouldn't be doing it at all unless we had a wish to get to the other place. When Rudyard Kipling's soldier complained that "there ain't no busses runnin' from the Bank to Mandalay", he did so only because he had a wish to go "back to Mandalay where the flyin'-fishes play, an' the dawn comes up like thunder outer China 'crost the Bay" and where he hoped still to find "a Burma girl a-settin'".

It is never *rational* to do anything whatever save to achieve some end which is *desired*. Reason itself is not a motive force within the personality: emotion alone is the motive force. (As the eighteenth-century philosopher David Hume put it in his *Treatise on Human Nature*: "Reason is, and ought only to be, the slave of the passions, and can never pretend to any other office than to serve and obey them.") And this is the moment to explain that I am using the word "emotion" in the widest possible sense, so as to include, in fact, everything which *does* motivate us. And emotion, in this wide sense, may be unconscious rather than conscious, or at least have origins which are unconscious rather than conscious.

Of course philosophers who write about free will must necessarily have an emotional urge to do so. This in itself is not the problem: they might still treat the subject with nothing but rationality. The trouble, it seems to me, is that very often they don't. They may have been attracted to it in the first place because they have an acknowledged or unacknowledged axe to grind; and even if this is not so, they will be exceptional if they approach it with complete disinterest. The philosopher Daniel Dennett, for example, has said [2]:

> When we consider whether free will is an illusion or reality, we are looking into an abyss. What seems to confront us is a plunge into nihilism and despair.

Well, if you really *feel* like that you're going to look for a way of escape – a way to draw back from the abyss – and Dennett does so. My point, of course, is that the sense of being plunged into nihilism and despair is not a rational, inevitable or universal reaction to the idea that free will is an illusion, as Dennett seems to suggest, but rather an individual, subjective and emotional one. Along with many other people, I don't share it.

In *NFW* [3] I had a look at the approach of Robert Kane, another philosopher who has an avowed wish to validate free will. He seeks to uphold it through his theory of "self-forming actions" and I tried to suggest that this idea just doesn't stand up to scrutiny. Other philosophers try to achieve the same end in their own different ways. I'm not suggesting (perish the thought) that philosophers who try to uphold free will are being in any way dishonest. Even if they are aware of their emotional attachment to it, and they may not be, they are almost certainly unaware of the origins of the attachment – of what the idea of free will *means* to them. And I'm not suggesting either that, when they seek to construct and marshal arguments in favour of some species of free will, they are being consciously disingenuous. Almost certainly they suppose, as they formulate and express their thoughts, that they are being as rational as the day is long.

In actual fact, of course, philosophers who try to uphold free will don't always spend any time at all in constructing and marshalling arguments in favour of it, because they don't see free will as something that needs to be explained or justified – any more than you or I would see the need to explain or justify love or hate or a fear of death. Free will, to them, is just something taken for granted, something they think they somehow experience, something they seem to *feel*; and their efforts are directed, not to explaining or justifying it, but only to repelling attacks upon it. Attacks come usually through the concept of determinism, and if some hole can be picked in that concept (for example, by resort to the indeterminacy of quantum mechanics) they think that free will has been saved, no matter how incoherent the concept of free will itself might prove to be if they felt the need to analyse it.

I realise that I take my life in my hands by suggesting that much of the philosophy of free will is just not rational. But look: surely there is no real room for doubt or argument about the underlying facts: the facts are out there. Does anyone seriously doubt that our biological inheritances combine with our environmental experiences to make us the people we are? Does anyone seriously doubt that we behave as we do because we *are* the people we are? I don't think so. Yet philosophers of free will seem collectively to resemble the character invented by the writer Stephen Leacock, who "jumped upon his horse and rode off madly in all directions".

There must be something – mustn't there? – there really must be *something* which accounts for this remarkable diversity in the drawing of conclusions from largely undisputed and rather simple facts. Because pure reason – logic, rationality – is surely what Shakespeare (perhaps mistakenly) said love was: an ever-fixed mark. 1+1 is always going to be 2; the price of four hot cross buns is always going to be four times the price of one (unless there's a special offer); and any two chains of thought which start in the same place are bound to end in the same place if the links are forged by pure reason. Forgive the mechanistic analogy, but if you feed the same facts into two computers programmed in the same way you'll get the same two answers. And if different *people* follow these chains of thought they are always going to get the same answers unless they get the answers "wrong", and they are not going to get them wrong unless they lack the capacity (the intelligence, if you like) to get them right. And, by the same token, any two philosophers who start from the same factual premises are always going to reach the same conclusions *if* the reasoning powers of both are up to scratch and *if* both are guided solely by reason. The trouble is that, where voyages of philosophical discovery are concerned, pure reason is not the star to every wandering bark.

There was a time in my life when I was much preoccupied with Freud and psychoanalysis. I certainly wouldn't stake what remains of my life on the correctness of all Freud's theories, but I would willingly stake it on the importance of the unconscious mind (or the unconscious brain, if you prefer) as a cause of human behaviour because this is increasingly confirmed by neuroscience. In a book aimed at the general reader, *Our Necessary Shadow: the Nature and Meaning of Psychiatry* [4], the psychiatrist Professor Tom Burns says:

> Freud's 'fanciful theory' of the power of the unconscious is being richly confirmed by neuroscientific research, although the accumulating evidence is that these unconscious processes underpin our healthy functioning, not just make us neurotic. All of us, not just those with psychiatric problems, are constantly at the mercy of our unconscious mental processes ... These determine our wellbeing and our mood much more than we had ever previously recognised. A wonderful irony is that so many of these findings are made by the very scientists who would be the fiercest critics of Freudian psychotherapy.

Actually, of course, Freud never thought that the unconscious was confined to processes that "just make us neurotic", and the importance of unconscious processes would have been "recognised" a lot sooner if "we" had listened to him in the first place; but never mind. (Though do, by the way, note Professor Burns's use of the word "determine".)

Another psychoanalytic concept which is accepted so widely as to have become commonplace is that of "rationalisation". It was introduced into psychoanalysis in 1908 by Dr. Ernest Jones, the first British analyst and the author of the three-volume biography of Freud, *Sigmund Freud: Life and Work* [5]. He described it as "the inventing of a reason for an attitude or action the motive for which is not recognised" – not recognised, that is, because it is unconscious. The fact that people rationalise their feelings in this way is a matter of everyday experience.

It does seem to me that putting these two concepts together and applying them to philosophers of free will goes a very long way towards explaining the differences in their approaches and their conclusions. Even if, as I suggest, there is only a single set of largely undisputed facts, there are as many different sets of unconscious motivations as there are people in the world and there are almost as many different ways of rationalising them. It is certainly hard to resist the idea that some philosophers, rather than following strictly rational chains of thought wherever they may lead, are striving for emotional reasons towards a goal which they have already set themselves [6]. So may I make one last suggestion which, particularly coming from a non-philosopher, may be thought quite outrageous? It's this: when philosophers adopt an idea or a position simply because they like it or find it congenial, or reject one simply because they don't like it or find it uncongenial ... that is the moment when they stop behaving as philosophers. After that, they become advocates, motivated not by clients' fees but by their own emotions.

I've already hinted that one of the stratagems which philosophers adopt in their quest to uphold free will is to re-define "free will" itself, doing so sometimes by stages and sleight of hand and perhaps in the hope that no one will notice what's going on. This ploy deserves a chapter to itself.

3

Accept no substitutes

Free will philosophy and sleight of hand

All that free will requires, according to [compatibilists] is that people are free to do what they choose to do: the fact that their choices are determined ... does not seem to these philosophers to matter. (NFW, p. 16)

Having written the last chapter, I laid my tools aside and read a book by Julian Baggini called *Freedom Regained: the Possibility of Free Will* [1]. I wanted to find a recent example to back up some of the things I said at the end of that chapter and I thought this book might provide it.

So it did; and oddly enough there is even some support in it for what I said there about different philosophers being driven by their different motivations (conscious or unconscious) to reach different conclusions about free will [2]. Approvingly, Baggini quotes [3] the philosopher Tammler Sommers as saying:

> Philosophers working on free will and moral responsibility proceed almost exclusively by appealing to intuitions ... and then developing theories to accommodate those intuitions.

Accept no substitutes

This support is particularly appropriate because Baggini himself is surely a prime example of someone whose arguments are angled towards a conclusion at which he wishes to arrive. It's hard to believe that he would have *wanted* to write a book in which he was led to condemn the idea of free will hook line and sinker: his drive and thrust is always towards preserving some version or vestige of it, and he is obviously pleased to think that he has managed to do so. There is an unexamined presupposition here that free will is a good thing to have and to believe in.

Many people will remember the old conjuring trick involving the smashed watch. The conjuror would borrow a valuable watch from someone in the audience – a gold fob watch would do nicely – wrap it in a handkerchief and, to the owner's horror, smash it to bits with a hammer. After some distractions and a lot of byplay, the conjuror would produce the watch from some unexpected place, show it to be intact and hand it back, to the relief of the owner and the applause of the audience. Baggini, it seems to me, does much the same thing with free will – but there's an important difference. In the conjuring trick, of course, the watch didn't really get smashed at all: the conjuror concealed it by sleight of hand, smashed something else in the handkerchief, and so was able to give the watch back unharmed. Baggini does the trick differently because he really does start by smashing the watch – or rather the normal, popular, mainstream version of free will – and in his case the subsequent distractions and byplay serve to obscure the fact that what he eventually hands back, though he calls it free will, is nothing like the thing he's smashed.

Let's remind ourselves of the essence of what I am calling mainstream free will [4]. This is the version which nearly everyone believes in, the version which underlies our justice system [5], the version which (going back to Chapter 1) would mean that Burglar Bill might not break into the apparently empty house, that Hitler might not have dedicated himself to war or Mandela to peace, the

The Cruelty of Free Will

version which, as I tried to show in *NFW*, is the only one capable of bearing the weight we put on it. I do very slightly resent the need to describe it as a "version" at all because, from where I'm standing (and I'm standing in the august company of a lot of philosophers) this is what free will is supposed to be. It consists in the idea that people who are sane and not coerced could and might have acted on any given occasion in ways different from those in which they did act.

This is the free will which results from an affirmative answer to the "Could he have done otherwise?" question. The question is usually worded like this and I shall stick with this wording but, as I've already suggested (and as I tried to explain in more detail in *NFW* [6]), it's very important not to misunderstand its meaning. To ask this question is not to ask whether the person was physically capable of doing otherwise, but rather to ask whether, *while being the same person in the same situation, he really might have done otherwise*. And only if the answer is Yes can mainstream free will be said to exist. In common with many others, I believe that the answer must clearly be No, and that's what makes me call free will a nonsense concept. I tried to show in *NFW*, and to recapitulate in Chapter 1 of this book, the way in which this free will is destroyed by determinism (or causality): the fact that every event has a cause, and every cause is itself the effect of a prior cause, so that there are chains of causality, already in train before our births, which run on into our genetic endowments, run on into our upbringings and all the influences we meet throughout our lives, run on to create our characters (or our brains if you prefer) ... and run on, because they don't stop there and can't stop there, to *determine* the ways in which we behave. We behave as we do because of the factors, all of them originally external to ourselves, that have produced us.

Now, here's the thing. Baggini really does smash this version of free will – smashes it to bits time and again – and he also makes it clear that he accepts determinism. This might not seem the most promising of platforms on which to construct any meaningful version of free will, but he believes that he has succeeded in doing so. I have made a sustained attempt to study Baggini's book. This task has taken me far longer than it should have done because I have found myself constantly seeking distractions from it and excuses for postponing it and, although my desk in now littered with well over fifty pages of notes, I'm still not at all sure that I have managed to make any real sense of the book or even that there is any real sense to be made. But I think it's important not to give up at this point because Baggini's book has been quite well received and a proper exploration of his approach, tedious though it may prove to be, will shed some real light on one kind of free will philosophy and show the sort of thing that free will deniers like me are up against.

So take it step by step. Let's be sure, first of all, that Baggini really does smash the mainstream free will described above. He says:

> It rests on a naïve and simplistic assumption that we can rise above our biology and our history to make choices in a condition of unrestrained freedom. [7]

> [W]ho we are appears to be a product of *both* nature and nurture, in whatever proportions they contribute, *and nothing else*. In accounting for who we are, nature + nurture = 100 per cent. You are shaped by forces beyond yourself, and you do not choose what you become. And so when you go on to make the choices in life that really matter" [or, surely, the ones that don't] "you do so on the basis of beliefs, values and dispositions that you did not choose. In that sense, your choice is not fundamentally free because you could not have become other than the person you are. Although this may appear troubling, it is hard to see how it could be any other way. [8]

> [A] ... reason why at the moment of choice we cannot do otherwise is that we cannot be other than who we are, and so the idea that we are radically free to do anything at all makes no sense. The nature of the chooser is the key determinant of choice: *who we are* comes first and *what we do* follows. [9]

> Unfettered freedom is not only an illusion; it makes no sense. It would not be desirable even if we could have it ... The scientific world view, therefore, destroys only a straw-man version of free will, a naïve conception that would crumble under rational scrutiny long before scientists could get their hands on it. Quite simply, the commonplace idea of free will we have lost was always wrong. Good riddance to it. [10]

The italics in these extracts are Baggini's own. And all the extracts come, of course, as music to my ears. As a card-carrying denier of free will, I would agree wholeheartedly with what he says. More music is supplied by his demolition of the idea of "origination", which I sought to demolish in *NFW* [11]. This is the idea that human beings have within themselves some facility (a "prime mover unmoved") which is the cause or origin of our behaviour but which is not itself caused by anything. Of this Baggini says:

> What it adds up to is simply the proposal that human beings have some power to cause things to happen which is independent of all forms of natural causation. In other words, it's free will by magic. [12]

Other extracts could be quoted, but let's pass on to Baggini's acceptance of determinism. This is implicit in some of the extracts above, but it is explicit in others:

> The computer analogy may be overworked when it comes to the brain, but there is a sense in which all your beliefs and desires are now part of a program, the software that runs on the hardware of the brain. Given all this, surely it is not open to the brain to generate just any response? Indeed, it is bound to generate only one. [13]

> Human actions flow as inexorably from the characters of the actors as water flows inexorably from the source of a river. The

only reason why we do not acknowledge this is that we do not feel any compulsion to act as we do. Our actions appear optional to us because the forces that make them inevitable are not evident to us. [14]

These extracts too come as music to my ears, because they too echo the thoughts I tried to express *NFW*. We need to notice next Baggini's response to the "Could he have done otherwise?" question. Several of the extracts quoted above make it clear that his answer (like mine) is No, and that it proceeds from his acceptance of determinism; but this is a particularly important matter and a couple more extracts will do no harm:

> [A]t any set point, we cannot do other than what we in fact do. To claim otherwise is to claim that we can defy the laws of nature, make physical objects immune to physical causes. [15]
>
> At the moment of any choice, the one you made was the only one you could have made. The feeling that you could have done otherwise is illusory. [16]

But now comes the moment we've been waiting for. In the light of all this, what version of free will can it be that Baggini thinks he has established? One point should be mentioned at the outset. Despite the unequivocal clarity of the extracts set out above, he seems quite often to feel an urge to water them down. For example (the italics are mine this time) he speaks in other parts of the book of there being "*some important sense* in which we could not have done otherwise" [17]; of our abilities being "*in one sense* simply the result of nature and all past experience" [18]; of the choices we make being "*from a certain point of view*" the only ones possible [19]; and of it being true that "*in some sense* people could not have done other than as they did" [20]. We are never told in what "sense" or from what "point of view" these things might not be so, and these intermittent fudges form no part of his argument, so I say no more about them: but I think that they arise from some unconscious uneasiness on his part. This uneasiness seems to reach its climax in some strange attempts at thought-policing, when he says that people shouldn't "*focus too much* on the *sense in which* they could not have done otherwise" [21] and indeed that they should not even "stop and ask" whether they could have done otherwise because this "*is a thought too many*" [22]. The justification for these moral prohibitions is not disclosed.

So what about Baggini's free will? From the title of his book you might think that he is not asserting that any kind of free will actually exists – only that it is a "possibility". But this would be quite wrong. He really does believe that he has established a version of free will – he calls it "a reformed free will" [23] – and indeed that there *is* no version but his. In his view not merely is mainstream free will nonsensical (I'm with him there), but all those who think, as I do, that the only version of free will which deserves the name must *be* mainstream free will (and many philosophers do think exactly that) are "in the midst of a thicket of misconceptions" and misled by "myths". To him free will "is neither what it is usually thought to be nor what many want it to be" [25]. So what does he think it is?

It is, he says, "partial, not absolute" [26], but what does this mean? It is meaningless to call something "partial" unless there is a whole for it to be a part of: Baggini's whole is what he calls "absolute" free will, and by this he can only mean the mainstream free will that I've tried to describe. So what *part* of mainstream free will is *his* free will? He dismisses mainstream free will as a thicket of misconceptions and myths, so what section, piece or aspect of it is he nonetheless adopting as his own? I wish I knew. But I shall set out a number of the things he says about his free will (I'll call it Baggini free will, of "BFW" for short – but for goodness' sake don't confuse this with *NFW*, my abbreviation for my earlier book) in case you can work it out for yourself. Those old enough to remember the American satirical soap opera *Soap* may recall the catchphrase which ended the opening plot summaries: "Confused? You will be!"

> *BFW is something we ourselves must strive to create.* It "is not something either present or absent, but something we have in degrees. You build your freedom step by step…" [27] "What we are doing when we set out to think about free will … is to find out what we must do to make it real." [28] "A well-developed free will is not a universal gift from birth but an achievement we need to strive for" [29] although "our freedom is extremely limited" [30]. (As a determinist, of course, Baggini would accept that the amount of BFW that we have, the extent to which we strive for more of it, and the success or failure of our strivings, are all the result of determinism. This doesn't seem to him to matter.)

> *BFW is self-control.* "What makes us free is that, taken in the round, we have a sufficient amount of control over what we do." [31] "We have something deserving the name of free will just as long as there is a meaningful sense in which we are in control of what we think and do". [32] "[R]eal free will … is in essence 'A healthy control system where all the bits are working well'." [33] "All free will requires from science is confirmation that human beings are self-organising, self-regulating organisms whose conscious beliefs, desires and deliberations affect their actions." [34] "To be free is not always to be in conscious control, but it does require a critical role for the conscious mind" [35]. As against this, however, "to insist free choice always requires conscious deliberation is to demand more than even our subjective experience suggests we need" [36] and "[m]any of our choices are made automatically or unconsciously, yet they are still free." [37] (It would be rash to suggest that these statements are consistent. And some of them seem to embody the idea of "origination" which Baggini has rejected.)

> *BFW is the ability to choose (even though there's only one thing we can choose).* "What really seems to matter for the artist is not that she could have chosen other than she did, but that she can choose

other than what others would choose for her or for themselves. To put it another way, the freedom desired is the freedom to do as you do, not to do other than you might have done [*sic*. Surely he means 'other than you do'?]." [38] "You do not achieve freedom by being the author of your own preferences and wants. You find freedom by being able to reflect on, endorse and express those preferences and wants." [39] (But of course you are no more the author of your ability to do this.) "A person who is more informed and educated has more capacity to make choices for herself, and therefore has a more developed free will." [40] "We cannot easily control what we want, but we can decide to act on those wants or not." [41] (And this from an avowed determinist!) "To say that [a choice] was free is to say that it is a choice you made without coercion, on the basis of values and beliefs you endorse." [42] On the other hand, "[e]ven our free choices can be in some sense mysterious to those who make them" [43] and "it is not bad faith to accept that our choices are very much constrained by our biological, psychological and social pasts and presents." [44] (The suggestion that they are not completely so constrained is another strange idea from a determinist, and one which seems to contradict assertions quoted earlier in this chapter.)

BFW is being yourself. "[H]owever paradoxical it sounds, there is a freedom in being able to run along your own rails, not to have to follow tracks which others push you into." [45] "[W]hat seems to be central [to free will] is autonomy and lack of coercion, an ability to act free from the prescriptions of others and of convention." [46] "To be free is for one's decisions, actions, beliefs and values to be one's own." [47] "Freedom can ... be understood as the capacity to live and act entirely according to your true nature." [48] Free will is " 'having the will I have, being the person I want to be' " [49].

BFW is having no conflicting motivations. Baggini emphasises the philosopher Harry Frankfurt's idea that we can have "first-order" and "second-order" desires [50]. We might want another piece of cake, but also (because we're on a diet) want not to want it: to you and me this is simply to have conflicting motivations, but let's not rain on Frankfurt's philosophical parade. Baggini endorses Frankfurt's view that to have free will is simply to be free of such conflicts: "[W]e ... can live as free agents so long as we want our wants, value our values and so do what we want to want to do." [51] Again, it is suggested that free actions are ones that flow from character, but that "[c]haracter in this sense is only possessed by those who have achieved a harmony of first- and second-order desires" which makes free will "a rare achievement". [52]

BFW is the ability to do better next time. "We might accept that, at the moment of action ... a person could not have done otherwise" but "[t]he point about holding them responsible is not about looking back to what is done and dusted, but ... making them realise that they could and should do better in future." [53] "To say someone has free will is to say that they are capable of modifying their own behaviour". [54] "[T]he real point of thinking 'I could have done otherwise' is 'I could do otherwise in similar future situations'." [55] "The feeling that you could have done otherwise is illusory. But this does not mean that it [*sic*. What is "it"?] was not free. To say it was free is to say ... that you have the general capacities to make alternative choices at other times." [56] (But of course future choices soon become past choices and, like past choices, are the only ones you could have made.)

Well, that's it. Some of these six conditions (or definitions or features, call them what you will) seem to have internal contradictions. Be that as it may, the real question is: how do they stand in relation to one another? Quite clearly they are not different ways of saying the same thing, but ways of saying quite different things. Is the existence of any one of them enough by itself to constitute BFW? Clearly not: the mere fact of being yourself, for instance, can hardly amount to BFW if none of the other conditions is met. So probably they must all be met if BFW is to arise. But if BFW does not exist unless you "strive" for it (something which I for one have never thought to do)

The Cruelty of Free Will

and it's "extremely limited" *and* it's a "rare achievement", it seems unlikely that many people possess it to any degree, or indeed at all. I myself have spent most of my life saddled with first- and second-order desires, so I'm disqualified on that score too. BFW seems to be a sort of will-o'-the wisp which Baggini chases hither and thither, but whose fitness for the role he never really tries to establish. I say this because there is no actual *reasoning* behind any of these six conditions: none of them generates free choice, and the idea that they amount, either singly or in combination, to anything that should be called free will is supported by nothing beyond Baggini's bald, unsupported and unargued assertion that they do. The ability to do better next time, for example, is possessed by nearly everyone; it has an obviously deterministic explanation (because past experience is a causal influence on future behaviour); and it could certainly be described as a jolly good thing; but what qualifies it to play a part in upholding the idea of "free will"?

Anyone conscientious enough to have read the whole of this chapter is likely to be in a bad mood by now. Isn't all this detail inexpressibly boring, and aren't I overloading the book by spending so much time with Baggini? I understand these feelings because I share them, but I shall try to explain. Although I did feel a certain wide-eyed incredulity on first reading his attempts to uphold free will, Baggini is actually not untypical of a class of "compatibilist" philosophers, all of whom try to do this by asserting that free will is somehow compatible with determinism. In seeking to show that his own attempt to pull off this trick leads only to incoherence – something which I could not have done without going into this degree of detail – I am trying to make a wider point about compatibilism in general: that it must always and necessarily founder in this sort of way.

All through the writing of this chapter, I've been plagued by a couple of lines from Rudyard Kipling's poem *Gehazi*. The poem was aimed at Rufus Isaacs, a barrister who, as Attorney General, was

Accept no substitutes

involved in the Marconi scandal and accused of corruption. He was cleared, but Kipling would have none of it and when Isaacs became Lord Chief Justice he likened him to the biblical character Gehazi [57] and aimed a missile at him in the shape of this poem. It begins:

"Whence comest thou, Gehazi,
    So reverend to behold,
In scarlet and in ermines
    And chain of England's gold?"
"From following after Naaman
    To tell him all is well,
Whereby my zeal hath made me
    A Judge in Israel."

The rest of the poem was blistering, but it did Isaacs no harm: he went on to become Marquess of Reading and Viceroy of India. And the lines that keep occurring to me are, "From following after Naaman to tell him all is well". Anyone who surrenders to Baggini the watch of mainstream free will doesn't get it back in any form at all – I'm still wondering in what possible sense BFW can amount to "partial" mainstream free will – but this is where the analogy breaks down (as analogies do) because people know exactly what their watches look like but they really don't know what free will looks like. It's just something which underpins and justifies their established attitudes, so when someone like Baggini – a compabilist – comes along to tell them all is well, they're only too pleased.

4

What's in a name?

The disputed meanings of "free will"

We need to bear in mind what Humpty Dumpty said "in a rather scornful tone" in Alice Through the Looking-Glass: "When I use a word it means just what I choose it to mean – neither more nor less." (NFW, p. 17)

At the end of the last chapter I suggested that compatibilist philosophy like that of Julian Baggini tends to be welcomed because, although people in general don't concern themselves with the true nature of "free will", they still want to have it. They believe that it validates and justifies many of the things they think and do and want to go on thinking and doing, so they are glad to be offered anything which purports to shore it up. From where I'm standing, to say that you are a determinist but you still believe in free will is a bit like saying that you're an atheist but you still believe in God, or that you're a mathematician but you still believe that two and two make five. That's because the only kind of free will meaningful to me is mainstream free will. Baggini's free will, if it amounts to anything at all, amounts to something quite different and although, in a rare moment of self-doubt, he does wonder whether it deserves the name of free will, he decides that it does [1].

So this is really a dispute, not about facts, but about what the words "free will" *mean*. It's important to reiterate that philosophers and others who disagree about free will are not disputing the existence or non-existence of some clear and uncontroversial thing like a hammer or a handsaw, but are dancing around a concept which has no clear meaning at all. The phrase "free will" is in no way self-explanatory. No one supposes that there is some distinct entity (in the mind or in the brain) called the "will", and even if there were there is nothing in the phrase itself to indicate what its freedom is supposed to consist in or amount to.

The result is that anyone can draw attention to certain characteristics or attributes of human beings, the existence of which may be obvious and undisputed, and label them as "free will". Of course other people will then disagree as to whether they should or should not bear that label, but these disputes are not about matters of substance, not about facts. At bottom, they are disputes about the meaning of words – about the meaning to be given to a phrase which of itself doesn't *have* any clear meaning. You could even say that these disputes are not for philosophers at all, but for lexicographers – for the compilers of dictionaries. And yet ... well, this takes us back to Chapter 2 because although the disputes are about the meanings of words, they are *fuelled* by the emotions which the disputants bring to bear upon them. If we really could take the emotion out of free will philosophy then, and only then, could the questions at issue be settled by lexicographers.

Baggini's compatibilist approach avowedly rejects what I have called mainstream free will. He maintains that his free will (whatever exactly it is) exists even though, on the face of it, he gives a clear No answer to the "Could he have done otherwise?" question. I say "on the face of it" because, as I suggested in the previous chapter, there are passages in his book which seem to show some unacknowledged equivocation about this, as if he isn't really very happy to commit himself to what he's saying. This is understandable. To quote from a book to which I shall want to return later on, James B. Miles's *The Free Will Delusion: How we Settled for the Illusion of Morality* [2]:

> [The philosopher] Bruce Waller has shown better than anyone [that] when you scratch beneath the surface of compatibilism you rarely find a wholehearted rejection of belief in ... free choice. It appears that compatibilists ... often lack the desire to consistently and continuously recognise the absence of free choice.

Miles refers [3] also to the strange results to which compatibilist philosophy can sometimes lead. The compatibilist philosopher Daniel Dennett, for example, has suggested that the Viking spacecraft had free will as soon as NASA stopped directing it. Miles suggests that, on Dennett's formulation, a toy car set to race away has free will if you walk off and leave it to its own devices, and that free will is possessed also by yeast and chrysanthemums.

So the meaning of the phrase "free will" is up for grabs and it can be given meanings which justify the conclusions of Baggini or Dennett or anyone else. Then why go on about it?, you may say: if compatibilists think they've got free will, and want us to think we've got free will, what does it matter? It takes all kinds to make a world: leave them alone and let them get on with it. But no one who cares about the human condition – about humanity itself – can afford to do that because there really is an issue here and it's a deeply important one. As I've already suggested, the idea that we have free will underlies many human attitudes which are abhorrent and is thought to justify many kinds of human behaviour which are cruel. I plan to say more about that later on. For now I want to nail some colours to the masthead.

What matters, and matters very much indeed, is not whether the meaning of "free will" can be stretched so as to embrace being yourself, or being single-minded, or being well-educated, or being able to tie your own shoelaces, but whether we have any sort of

What's in a name?

capacity or facility to act in ways different from those in which we do act. Might we really do otherwise? Might my Burglar Bill really turn away and go home? Might Hitler really have turned out a nice man and Mandela a monster? I say No. Baggini says No. And I know of no one who has thought about it – certainly no determinist – who says Yes. This is what matters to us as members of the human race. Mainstream free will is the thing that matters, and we haven't got it. We haven't created ourselves, and we have no choices that are free from causality. If it were possible to detach the clear and almost undisputed central *fact* that kills mainstream free will – the fact that outside circumstances have created us and programmed us to do what we do – from the vague, amorphous and much disputed general *concept* of "free will", that would be a huge blessing. I sometimes hanker for trying to give free will another, clearer, more self-explanatory name (simply "free choice" perhaps?), but of course it isn't possible. We're stuck with the idea of "free will", stuck with its lack of clarity and stuck with the fact that any incoherent version of it can be called in aid to justify our continued lack of understanding, our continuing cruelty.

5

A short trip to Frankfurt

An example of philosophical sophistry

[D]esultorily, at an abstruse level and
inconclusively, the arguments go on.
As I read more about them I found myself
lost in wonder at the sophistry with which
the issues were treated or, much more
often it seemed to me, avoided. (NFW, p. 2)

Most of us like an occasional holiday break and this chapter is meant to provide one. The philosopher Harry Frankfurt was mentioned in Chapter 3 in connection with his idea that we may have first- and second-order desires, and that to have free will is not to have any of the latter [1]. But Frankfurt provides another diversion worth exploring.

In the last chapter I claimed that the only kind of free will that merits the name – the only one that really matters to us – is free choice. This is the mainstream free will which depends on a Yes answer to the "Could he have done otherwise?" question. But Frankfurt has proposed thought experiments which purport to show that we can have free will – even mainstream free will – despite a No answer to this question.

In essence a Frankfurt thought experiment runs like this. Imagine a scenario in which a mad scientist is somehow able to experiment on a human being. We'll call her Mimi. In real life, Mimi is faced with the need to act in one of two different ways and has to choose between them. The scientist wants her to act in one particular way and not the other. He has implanted a device in her brain which tells him how she intends to act if left to herself. And the device also enables him to compel her to act in the way he wishes. In actual fact, the device tells him that she herself will act in just the way he wants her to act, so he sits back and does nothing and Mimi goes ahead without interference.

The point of this thought experiment? Well it shows, according to Frankfurt, that whether Mimi could have done otherwise is irrelevant to the question of whether she had free will. Of course, if the scientist had divined that Mimi was about to make the wrong choice and forced her to make the right one, not even the most staunch believer in free will would suggest that Mimi had exercised her own free will in making this choice, or that she should be held responsible for it. That isn't the point. The point is that, as things turned out, the scientist didn't intervene at all, and yet – wait for it – she still couldn't have done otherwise because he would have stopped her. In this strange scenario there was in actual fact (though she didn't know it) no alternative possibility open to her. Yet she did exactly what she would have done if she'd never met the wretched scientist. So if – if – her choice would otherwise have been an expression of free will, it would still have been an expression of free will even though she "couldn't have done otherwise". See? And if you generalise this result, you're supposed to conclude that free will simply doesn't depend on the ability to do otherwise.

Believe it or not, this thought experiment has occupied a lot of philosophers' time. They've mulled over it, developed it and produced refined versions of it – and all, it seems to me, without appreciating that it is based on pure semantics, mere word-play. When people like me ask the "Could he have done otherwise?" question, what we want to know is whether human beings are or are not constituted in a particular way. What we are asking is whether, faced with a choice between two alternatives, people are by the states of their *own characters* (the states of their own natures, their own brains) constrained to choose a particular one and not the other, or whether they have *within themselves* some faculty or facility such that they really might choose either. The theoretical possibility that some external agent might prevent them from choosing one of the two alternatives is surely quite irrelevant. Is it actually possible that my Burglar Bill, by virtue of his *own* nature, his *own* character, his *own* personality – call it what you will – might decide to break in, or might equally well decide to go home instead? No it isn't, and that's what rules out mainstream free will. It is certainly not ruled back in again by the fact that, unknown to him, some external influence might in theory have prevented him from choosing the alternative which he had no wish to choose.

Yet this is exactly the kind of sophistry with which free will philosophy is so often beset. It serves as a kind of fog in which people lose their way, going round in circles, finding themselves back at their starting point and never getting to the true destination – a destination which amounts in my view to a plain and simple rejection of any meaningful kind of free will. Those who produce the fog may not want them to reach this destination, and those who get lost in the fog may be only too glad not to reach it.

6

Free will and hypocrisy

How we accept determinism in all but name

There is nothing new in the idea that people can harbour two diametrically opposed beliefs at the same time, acting in some circumstances on the one and in other circumstances on the other. (NFW, p. 71)

What most people think that they possess — and think that those they love and those they hate possess — is freedom of choice: mainstream free will. But although they cling tenaciously to this belief, they are happy to see it contradicted every day. Part III of my *NFW* was called "Do we really believe in free will?" and the answer I tried to give was that we do and we don't [1]. We "believe" in it when it suits us emotionally to do so; but when it doesn't, we forget all about it. I pointed out that the existence of mainstream free will would be inconsistent with the sciences (psychology, psychiatry, criminology and all the rest) which concern themselves with human behaviour, because if free choice existed it would sever the connection between ourselves as people and the ways in which we behave — between who we are and what we do. Our behaviour would not reveal our characters, our characters would not show forth in our behaviour, and it would not be relevant to consider how we came to have the characters we have.

Like all scientific investigations, whatever their subject, these ones assume and depend upon the existence of causality, and they could not possibly be pursued if they didn't. (And this, by the way, is surely true even in the microscopic world of quantum mechanics: it is precisely the apparent absence of causality which makes it inexplicable.)

By accepting the validity of these scientific explorations of the human condition we contradict our belief in free choice. And our tacit acceptance of causality in human affairs goes much wider than this. Whenever a human being does something remarkable, especially if it is something bad, we are sure to find in the media attempts at explanation or calls for explanation. Why did they do it? What went into the making of these evil people? Today, as I write this, there is coverage of the latest of the many mass shootings made possible by the gun culture of the United States. My newspaper tells me that the perpetrator was "overly-protected by his mother", that his father was "not in the picture" when he was born, that he was turned down by the Army, and so on. These things are mentioned only because they are thought to shed some light on him and what he did.

The idea of causality in human behaviour is inescapable. Over a short period I've collected a few examples:

> A consultant physician writing to *The Times* says that lead in petrol will cause an increase in violent crime: "Lead burden is most dangerous in utero and infancy, so high levels of exposure can be expected to manifest themselves in dysfunctional behaviour among teenagers and adults 20 years later."

> A newspaper headline: *Feeling stressed? Then blame your mother.* This is because "stress [in the mother] makes the placenta more leaky, allowing cortisol to cross."

> Another newspaper headline: *Fat chance of obese returning to normal size, say experts.* This is because "research has suggested that evolutionary mechanisms designed to help humans stay at

their maximum sustained weight kick in to stop the obese losing weight."

A newspaper article about the late John Freeman asks: "Why was [he] so fanatically private, where did his ruthlessness come from?"

A review, having praised the posthumous book of a neurosurgeon who qualified while dying of cancer, ends by saying, "But from where does his obsession with work derive …?"

In a newspaper interview with the actor and author Simon Callow, he is asked, "Where does your love of biography come from?"

A newspaper headline about athletes: *What drives a man to run and run?*

A newspaper headline about alcoholism: *Found: gene that drives us to drink.*

The heading of a newspaper article: *The making of Jihadi John: What turned Mohammed Emwazi from wide-eyed British schoolboy into the Isis executioner?*

Another newspaper headline: *Regret when you lost your virginity? Blame your genes.*

A film director's reported comment about suicide bombers: "Instead of seeing these people just as psychopaths, we should ask what has made them so."

A newspaper article about Yehudi Menuhin reports his son as saying, "He didn't have moods. He was either more distant or less distant", and adds: "Psychologists will see a ready explanation for that".

The Cruelty of Free Will

A few of these quotes, or the text associated with them, purport to be to some extent explanatory of human behaviour. Others merely call for explanations. All of them assume that there *are* explanations. The point I'm making is that we read them with hardly a second thought. They don't offend us. No one condemns them on the ground that they are inconsistent with free will, but of course they are. I'm reminded of the quotation, "There are none so blind as those who will not see". And apparently there's a second half to this quotation which goes, "The most deluded people are those who choose to ignore what they already know". In the present context, this second part is more telling than the first. Aldous Huxley in *Brave New World*[2] makes rather the same point: "Great is truth, but greater still, from a practical point of view, is silence about truth."

Philip Larkin's best-known poem is the one that starts:

> They fuck you up, your mum and dad.
>   They may not mean to, but they do.
> They fill you with the faults they had
>   And add some extra, just for you.

Some people have objected to his language but no one, so far as I know, has said that he was wrong.

Recently I watched a television programme about police procedure. It involved a man who had been caught with pictures of child abuse on his computer. At the end of his interview, a police officer said she had one last question for him. "Explain to me." she said, "why you take sexual pleasure in a baby being raped." I fell to wondering what kind of explanation she was looking for. A psychological or psychoanalytical explanation might possibly be available, but obviously the offender wouldn't know what it was. And a neurological explanation probably exists in principle but, unless his paedophilia was caused by actual brain injury or disease [3], it will not be available in practice for many years, if ever. In fact, of course, the police officer was not seeking an explanation of either kind, and she would probably have rejected it if one had been given: she intended her question to be unanswerable, except perhaps in terms of the offender's "wickedness". The offender's actual reply showed a presence of mind which was unexpected in the circumstances: he said he didn't know, and asked her to explain why she took pleasure in normal sexual intercourse.

In 2007 a 17 month-old child who came to be known as Baby Peter died after suffering over fifty injuries. His mother, her boyfriend and the boyfriend's brother all went to prison. Sir Martin Narey made some comments about the case. He was formerly the Director General of the Prison Service and at this time he was Chief Executive of the charity Barnardo's. He was reported in the *Daily Mail* as saying that, if Baby Peter had survived, his deprivation would probably have made him an unruly teenager and that he would then have become "feral, a parasite, a yob, helping to infest our streets". Narey was criticised for saying this, but he had been misreported. What he'd really said was that we as a society tended to sympathise with victims of abuse so long as they were babies or toddlers but that our sympathy and understanding evaporated when they grew up; and he added that if Baby Peter's neglect and abuse had turned him into an unruly young man the press would have ignored these factors, rounded on him, and called him "feral" or a "yob". No one took exception to what Narey had really said, and people took exception to what he was reported as saying only because they thought that it showed some lack of sympathy for Baby Peter.

I could go on, but I hope I've said enough to show that, at least for much of the time, we're quite happy to ignore mainstream free will and to endorse causality (determinism). All the examples I've given take for granted the idea that human behaviour results from external factors and all of them deny implicitly the existence of free choice. Ah, you may say, but they don't deny the existence of *some* free choice. There may still be a little bit of free choice in there somewhere, and that little bit ... well, yes, now I come to think about it, that little bit is all we need to establish mainstream free will. But it isn't, and there is no "little bit". We really cannot have it both ways. Julian Baggini espouses the idea of "partial free will", but it surely leads him into incoherence and even he doesn't suggest that it provides a Yes answer to the "Could he have done otherwise?" question. The answer to this question cannot be equivocal: it must be either Yes or No. It cannot be "Yes, if ...": (Yes, if he'd wanted to – but he didn't; Yes, if something had happened to change his mind – but nothing did; Yes, if he'd had a higher IQ – but he hadn't; Yes, if (Baggini again) he'd been better educated or motivated to "strive" harder – but he wasn't). In truth, there can be no such thing as a mainstream free will which is "partial".

So we really do forget about our belief in mainstream free will when it suits us to do so, don't we? But when it doesn't suit us (and Narey is right to suggest that it doesn't suit us when we're dealing with feral yobs) that's a very different story, and one for later chapters. This book sets out to show how, and why, belief in free will persists, and this chapter (like the three before it) has to do with the *how*, because it's precisely this convenient temporary amnesia about our belief in free will which allows us to preserve it. We keep it tucked away, safely cocooned, out of sight and out of mind, unaffected by the contradictions that wash over it, until the time comes for us to make use of it once again, when it springs back to life unscathed and in all its supposed potency.

Here's a final quote to illustrate the ambivalence [4]. A judge is sentencing a schoolmaster convicted of filming pupils in the shower room and encouraging them to sexual activity. The judge says, "You are a man looking at a life that is now in ruins. It is a life reduced to rubble as a result of your fatal flaw." As a *result* of your fatal *flaw*: here's a causal explanation if ever there was one. But then, without missing a beat, the judge wipes it away with a cloth soaked in free will: "You are the author of your own misfortune and there can be little sympathy for you."

7

If you're not rich, blame yourself

The cruelty of free will belief

At the end of one episode [of a boys' adventure serial] Jack found himself in an appalling situation, tied hand and foot and trapped so securely that no one could see how he could possibly extricate himself. Readers awaited the next episode with trepidation, but when it came out it began with the words, "With one bound Jack was free …". (NFW, p. 117)

When I was very young schoolboy I used to go home on the school bus. At one point it had to take a very sharp, steep downhill bend forming part of a four cross way and, although sometimes the driver got round it in one go, he often had to reverse and take another shot at it, his engine pushed to its limits as it propelled the bus backwards up the hill in a series of jerks. A little way down from the crossroads was another sharp bend on which there was a coal merchant's yard. And in a street beside it children played. I remember the children as being dirty (as well they might have been, living beside a coal merchant), ill-clothed and sometimes shoeless. They were poor children. I compared their situation with my own far better one (far better materially at least) and the comparison disturbed me. How could this be right, and why was the world not right? But I didn't like being disturbed and I thought to myself (and this I remember clearly) that they could all have good lives because they could perfectly well become solicitors like my dad.

My only excuse for this is that I can't have been more than about six or seven years old at the time. In due course I grew up and came to see how wrong I was. There are many people who harbour such thoughts and they too grow up but, almost unbelievably, they never come to see how wrong they are. And this is because it suits them to believe, and to go on believing, in free will.

The American presidential candidate Herman Cain said in 2012: "If you don't have a job and you're not rich, blame yourself." His statement, aimed at the population at large, is of course stupid even on a superficial level: for everyone to be rich is a logical impossibility as well as a practical one. But at a deeper level – the level which concerns us here – it is vicious as well as stupid, because it is fuelled by the idiotic idea of untrammelled free choice. Cain seems actually to believe (and was certainly pandering to those who believe) that all of us can, and really might, cast off our natural endowments however disabling, our social status however low, our upbringings however abusive, our educations however inadequate, and all the other things that have built us to be the way we are – cast them off and soar above them, leaving them far behind. And that we have only ourselves – *only* ourselves – to blame if we don't.

In my *NFW* I tried to show that belief in mainstream free will leads us to treat criminals with undeserved and unproductive cruelty. I suggested also that the problem goes beyond crime and distorts our attitudes in other ways. But it wasn't until I read a book already mentioned – James B. Miles's *The Free Will Delusion: How we Settled for the Illusion of Morality* [1] – that I appreciated the full implications of this. The sad fact is that the idea of free will is constantly called in aid, explicitly or implicitly, as justification for the social status quo however unfair and unjust this may be. Sympathy and understanding for poor, deprived, inadequate, unintelligent and otherwise disadvantaged people is destroyed or much reduced – together, of course, with the obligation of others to do something about their plight – by the idea that they could have freely chosen to escape from their situation and have freely chosen not to do so. By the same token, those who have wealth, status, privilege and celebrity can attribute these things, not to the advantages of birth, upbringing, education, opportunity and sheer good fortune, but rather to an exercise of free will of which everyone else was just as capable as they. All positions in life are thus somehow *deserved*. It would do me no good if I allowed politics to gain a foothold in this book, but it is a fact that Herman Cain was a Republican candidate, and indeed the candidate of choice for the Tea Party, and that belief in free will correlates highly with right wing views. So does belief in retributory punishment: more of that later. Few of those whose views incline more towards the left would thank me for calling them determinists, but their views do seem to rely much less on the idea of free will.

I had a wealthy aunt who had strong defences against feeling sympathy for the poor. She maintained that those who sleep rough on the streets of London, wrapping themselves in sheets of newspaper when the weather is cold, do so (and here her tone would rise to an angry crescendo in order to drown out any lingering doubt) "because they *like* it". It's true, of course, that many such people are no longer capable of getting a job or of holding one down, and it might be more painful for them to try than to remain homeless and cold and hungry, but that's not the point: the point is that they didn't freely choose to be the way they are, and there's really no sense in which they like it.

The views of people such as Herman Cain and my aunt (and there are very many such people, perhaps a large majority) rest upon the idea of free choice – mainstream free will. I don't see how mainstream free will would justify these views anyway because I don't see it as a coherent concept, but let that pass. Compatibilist free will on the other hand – "free will" like that of Julian Baggini and Daniel Dennett

– doesn't purport to generate free choice at all and therefore can't provide this kind of justification. Or so you might think; but the reality is less simple. For one thing, of course, people in general don't distinguish between one version of free will and another: it's all the same to them, carries the same message, justifies the same injustice. But there's something else, and it's really rather strange.

It would of course be possible for compatibilists to say, "Well, we maintain that you have what we call free will, but our kind of free will doesn't give you any free choices and we're sorry if you're disappointed, but that's the way it is and we've nothing to add." This seems to me the most sensible position for compatibilists to take up (and some of them do so) because in reality compatibilists leave us as human beings in exactly the same place as outright deniers of free will (like me) leave us. Neither approach provides any escape from the plain fact that the quality of our lives is wholly determined by a biological and environmental lottery, that life is therefore intrinsically unfair, and that huge undeserved suffering exists as a result. But some compatibilists try to avoid this conclusion, just as I tried to avoid it when I saw the poor children playing beside the coal merchant's yard. Realising that they are vulnerable to the accusation that their kind of "free will" doesn't alleviate the unfairness – has none of the *potency* that mainstream free will purports to have – they try to fend off the accusation by arguing that the unfairness is only apparent, doesn't really exist or doesn't really matter. They are a little like Dr. Pangloss in Voltaire's *Candide*[2] who claimed repeatedly that all is for the best in the best of all possible worlds.

Julian Baggini seems at first to fall into this category, but then draws back a little as he tends to do. Although as a compatibilist his free will excludes free choice, he still seeks to justify our existing attitudes and existing forms of punishment, even retributory punishment. This is certainly a little Panglossian. But as he comes to the end of the book he does devote just a few lines to the fact that his compatibilist free will allows us no escape from life's lottery [3]. Saying, rather inelegantly, that we should not "ignore the extent to which our freedom is extremely limited", he adds:

> I think the state has a role trying to iron out some of the injustices that result from things over which people have no control or responsibility. It is not by our free will that we are born into rich or poor families, have high or low IQ, suffer from disabilities or inherit debilitating medical conditions. Nature does not dispense her gifts according to any principles of justice.

Although it falls some way short of a rallying cry, this comment is welcome. Its truth may be thought obvious but, as James Miles points out, there are other compatibilist philosophers who seem not to accept it. I owe the rest of this chapter largely to his book, which gives the subject a much more comprehensive treatment than I can.

Compatibilist philosophers who try to wipe away the unfairness of life's lottery do so mainly because they want to provide themselves and the rest of us with a justification for the way in which we treat our fellow human beings – for the judgmental attitudes we bring to bear upon them [4]. In particular, they want to uphold our existing idea of "moral responsibility" (about which I say more in the next chapter) and the satisfying blame games and cruelties which it purports to justify. Dr. Pangloss would be proud of them.

Miles quotes [5], for example, the comments of the philosopher Gary Watson about the American serial killer Robert Harris. Harris had been tortured by his sadistic father, hated by his mother (who blamed him for the beatings which the father gave to her), bullied by his schoolmates, and then put in a children's prison where, from the age of fourteen, he was repeatedly raped. Watson says:

> There is room for the thought [and that's a gem, isn't it?] that there is something 'in me' by virtue of which I would not have become a vicious person in Harris's circumstances. And if that factor were among my essential properties, so to speak, then that

difference between Harris and me would not be a matter of moral luck on my part, but a matter of who we essentially were...

It is indeed conceivable that if Watson had lived Harris's life he wouldn't have become vicious (though he certainly wouldn't have become a professor of philosophy either), but if that were so it would simply mean that the difference between them lay more in their biological endowments than in their environmental experiences [6]. And the quality of one's biological endowment is surely the clearest and best example of luck that you could find in a long day's march, but for Watson it seems that this kind of luck should be treated quite differently from environmental luck. If he and Harris had different biological endowments – such that Harris and his like could be corrupted by bad environments while Watson and his like would always be incorruptible – then that is an "essential" difference between them, and Watson thinks it only right to treat essentially different human beings in essentially different ways. (Try as I may, I can't help being reminded of the essential differences believed to exist between Jews and Aryans in Hitler's Germany.) Still speaking of Harris, Watson says [7]: "The sympathy toward the boy he was is at odds with outrage toward the man he is ... Each of these responses is appropriate". I think back to Sir Martin Narey's comment, made about Baby Peter and recorded in Chapter 6: that public sympathy for abused children evaporates when the abuse turns them into criminal adults. Narey thinks this is wrong. Watson thinks it's right. I'm with Narey.

Daniel Dennett is perhaps the prime example of a compatibilist philosopher driven to extraordinary lengths in an effort to justify the social status quo and to deny the importance of biological and environmental luck and the unfairness to which it leads. He asks [8], "Is [the system] fair enough not to be worth worrying about?" He replies, "Of course", and then he adds (get this): "After all, luck averages out in the long run." This last statement isn't a throwaway line: Dennett really meant it and has defended it. But surely, surely it is self-evidently the most copper-bottomed, thoroughgoing, unmitigated rubbish. *Of course* luck doesn't average out in the long run. How did the luck of Baby Peter average out? How did the luck of Robert Harris? Or that of his victims? When is the luck of a gay man born into a society that hates gays (or a country that executes them) going to average out? When will the luck of those born brain-damaged average out? The luck of the chronically disabled? The luck of the schizophrenic, the psychopathic? It's apparent to anyone with eyes to see that, even in a relatively civilised country like Dennett's America (and let's not even think about what happens in less civilised countries), the luck inherent in our heredity and environment very seldom averages out, that on the contrary it tends to accumulate and to ramify. And those whose luck has left them ill-equipped for life are cursed not only with this disadvantage but with the fact that society looks down on them and even blames them because of it, while those whose start in life equips them with the means and motivation to succeed are praised, and even praise themselves, for their success. Towards the end of 2015, the Labour Party of which Jeremy Corbyn had become leader was condemned in the media [9] as the party for "down and out losers", the party of the "undeserving". But what the "undeserving" really don't deserve, surely, is the biological and environmental luck which has made them the way they are and denied them the motivation and ability to change their lives – that and the condemnation which they receive as a result. In this context at least the Gospel of St. Matthew (13:12) is all too often right to say

> For whosoever hath, to him shall be given, and he shall have more abundance: but whosoever hath not, from him shall be taken away even that he hath.

Dennett has defended his position [10] by saying that the luck which averages out for the disadvantaged includes "compensatory" mechanisms (so for those born with cerebral palsy who get

The Cruelty of Free Will

wheelchairs and for the starving who get food banks, their luck has turned) and that, even if luck does not average out for absolutely everyone, it does – or rather, to use Dennett's own words, "it could" – average out for a high proportion, with the clear implication that the rest don't really matter.

As professors of philosophy, Watson, Dennett and others who think as they do have ended with winning tickets in the lottery of life, so perhaps one can understand what Miles [11] calls their desperation "to provide a moral justification for the moral (mis)behaviour of the vast majority of us". And no one should blame them for their good luck, any more than the unlucky should be blamed for their lack of it. We should remember, too, that their behaviour is determined and not freely willed, determined in their case by the drawing of lucky tickets, just as the behaviour of the less fortunate is determined by the drawing of very different ones. But surely they are prime examples of the philosophers described in Chapter 2 who try to argue their way towards a conclusion to which they are already emotionally committed [12]; and, when all appropriate allowances are made, it is impossible to admire their attempts to shrug off the sufferings of the unfortunate.

8

Moral responsibility and Martin Luther

The faulty foundations of retribution

[T]he concept of moral responsibility ... is important only because of what we take to be its implications – because of the consequences which seem to us to flow from it. In practice it is a sort of label which we stick on other people when we want to visit those consequences upon them. (NFW, p. 96)

Philosophers like those mentioned in the previous chapter, who try to deny or wipe away the ill-distributed luck which governs our lives, wish to justify not only the social status quo but also, and perhaps even more, the moral status quo – our prevailing ideas about responsibility, deserts, blame, retribution and so on. Some of the things they say are illustrations of Bruce Waller's assertion [1] that, although compatibilist philosophy rejects the idea of free choice, this idea is still to be found there if you scratch beneath the surface. Daniel Dennett, for example, has said [2]:

> Common wisdom has it that ... I have created and unleashed an agent who is myself ... I think this common wisdom is indeed wisdom.

Grammatically, of course, the first sentence makes no sense [3]. It cannot be understood except on the basis that there is a distinction between subject and object – between the "I" who creates and unleashes the agent, and the agent who is created and unleashed – but this distinction is nullified by the disclosure that the "agent … is myself". And it carries overtones not only of free choice (since it implies that there is something about the creating and unleashing of "myself" which "I" might not have done), but also of self-creation (since it asserts that "I" did create "myself") and of origination (since the "I" who does the creating must have logically have existed – uncreated – before it brought "myself" into existence by creating it). None of these implications can withstand examination, but the statement nonetheless casts strong light on Dennett's motivation and on one of the ends he seeks to achieve: that of justifying common ideas about "responsibility".

Responsibility means different things in different contexts: it's a palace of varieties. Four of these meanings are worth noting here. First of all, and most simply, you can be *actually responsible* – in the primary sense of being the person who did whatever it was that someone did. (Am I responsible for writing this book? Yes. If you throw it in the bin, are you responsible for doing so? Yes, you are. If a serial killer murders five people, is he responsible for that? Yes, he is – and even if he's as mad as a hatter and thinks he's ridding the world of demons, he's still responsible in this sense because it was he, and no one else, who did it.) Then again you can be *held responsible*. This happens if someone or some institution (a court, a jury) decides that it was you who did whatever it was – and let's hope they've got it right, but they could be wrong. Then you can *accept responsibility*. You do this if you decide to admit your responsibility, either because you really are actually responsible or because you decide that you ought to behave as if you were. (Julian Baggini [4] laments the erosion of the principle of "ministerial responsibility", whereby it was usual for a government minister to resign if there was a serious mistake in his or her department even if the minister had nothing to do with it: he thinks the erosion fosters "a responsibility-shirking culture".) And then you can, or you may not, *feel responsible*. This concept has to do with the emotions which you harbour in connection with the thing you did: positive ones if it was a good thing, negative if it was bad. It's possible, though rather sad and strange, to feel responsible even if you're not actually responsible (a mother whose son was murdered by an online contact says the guilt never leaves her: "I keep thinking if only we hadn't moved to England, if only I hadn't sent him to that school, if only he hadn't loved computers. It never stops." [5]). It's also possible to be actually responsible without feeling any responsibility at all (and this might be so if you happen to be insane). But most of us feel responsible when, and only when, we are actually responsible and, if we are responsible for doing something bad, our feelings of guilt, shame, regret or remorse are the products of a more or less normal conscience.

Although we need to note these different conceptions of responsibility, we need to note also that none of them necessarily corresponds with the conception which is at the heart of free will philosophy: *moral responsibility*. Moral responsibility, of course, is the kind of responsibility which is thought to justify acts of revenge and retribution – to make them *deserved*. If people are morally responsible for deliberate ill-doing then the blame [6], anger, hatred, contempt and condemnation which we visit upon them is righteous, and they deserve to be punished. Moral responsibility is what gives us the right, and *makes* it right, to treat them in this way. It seems to be accepted that free will of some kind is necessary to give rise to moral responsibility. So closely linked, indeed, are these two ideas that they seem often to be defined in terms of one another: free will is whatever it is that is necessary to generate moral responsibility, while moral responsibility is whatever it is that is generated by free will.

But this kind of circularity gets us nowhere, so we must pursue our search. What are the pre-requisites for moral responsibility? Certainly sanity is one: the serial killer who thinks he is ridding the world of demons is actually responsible but would not be considered morally responsible. And most people would say that a Yes answer to the "Could he have done otherwise?" question is another pre-requisite. On that basis, moral responsibility is generated by – and only by – mainstream free will, which is supposed to entail free choice and an absence of determinism. Two fairly simple propositions seem thus to emerge from the fog: one, that if you do a bad thing and you really might have done otherwise, you must be morally responsible for doing the bad thing; and two, that if you do the bad thing and you couldn't have done otherwise, you can't be morally responsible for doing it. But neither of these propositions is immune from attack.

I'm going to attack the first one myself. The problem with free choice, as I suggested in Chapter 1, is that would sever the connection between ourselves and our behaviour. Determinism does at least anchor our behaviour securely to our personalities – to our characters, to our being the people we are – whereas mainstream free will breaks the connection and would make our behaviour free-floating and intrinsically inexplicable. I don't begin to see how this would generate moral responsibility. If it really were open to me either to hit you over the head or to shake you by the hand, and I am so constituted as to have a courteous wish to shake your hand but I nonetheless hit you over the head, how can this act possibly be explained or attributed to me? You may think that this scenario is crazy, and so it is, but that's because free choice is crazy.

What about the second proposition: that if you couldn't have done otherwise because your act is determined, you can't be morally responsible for what you do? I myself would wholeheartedly support this proposition. But of course many compatibilist philosophers, despite believing in determinism, still want to uphold the popular attitudes and punitive reactions which moral responsibility is supposed to justify – the moral status quo – and this is where they find themselves in trouble.

Moral responsibility and Martin Luther

How *do* you defend the idea that people *deserve* to be condemned and punished for doing something which they couldn't have refrained from doing? Philosophers may attempt this difficult task either by subverting the idea of moral responsibility itself – suggesting that some other conception of responsibility *amounts* to moral responsibility – or else by suggesting that we don't need moral responsibility at all because some other conception does the job.

In a well-known argument [7], Dennett takes as his starting point the statement of Martin Luther, who rebelled against the Roman Catholic Church, nailing a list of his grievances, called the *Ninety-Five Theses*, to a church door in Wittenberg in 1517. Summoned to appear before the Diet of Worms in 1521, Luther refused to back down, saying, "Here I stand, I can do no other." Apparently it's doubtful whether Luther really nailed anything to a church door or said these words at all, but no matter. Dennett's point is that even if he did make this statement, and even if it was literally true and he really couldn't have done otherwise, he was still responsible in a sense which justifies the popular attitudes described above. Dennett says:

> [H]is declaration is testimony to the fact that we simply do not exempt someone from blame or praise for an act because we think he could do no other. Whatever Luther was doing, he was not trying to duck responsibility.

Dennett is of course right in his description of the moral status quo: we certainly do dish out praise and blame for behaviour without thinking whether the behaviour is determined. But that by itself doesn't prove that we are right to do so: it takes more to justify an attitude than the mere fact that it *is* an attitude. In any case (as I argued in my NFW [8]), there are good pragmatic reasons for bestowing praise and if not exactly blame, then at least disapproval, which have nothing to do with moral responsibility and rest simply on the need to foster good behaviour.

But surely Dennett is also engaged in some sleight of hand here. It's true enough that Luther ticked all the boxes for the varieties of "responsibility" set out earlier: he was actually responsible, he was held responsible (to his cost), he accepted responsibility and he felt responsible. But there's nothing in this to contradict the fact that his actions and feelings were wholly determined by biological and environmental luck. And so, from where I'm standing, these facts do not amount to moral responsibility or provide a substitute for it. In 1959, Ernest Gellner wrote a book called *Words and Things* [9]. It attacked the linguistic philosophy then in vogue at Oxford and Bertrand Russell provided an Introduction in which he allied himself with this attack. Russell said of linguistic philosophy:

> This consists [partly] in reasoning from the actual use of words to answers to philosophical problems ... Mr. Gellner quotes as an example ... what some, at least, of the linguistic philosophers regard as a solution to the free-will problem. When a man marries without external compulsion, we may say, "he did it of his own free will". There is, therefore, a linguistically correct use of the words "free will", and therefore there is free will. No one can deny that this is an easy way to solve age-old problems.

And surely Dennett is trying to solve the "responsibility" problem by much the same means.

Julian Baggini's book provides another example of compatibilist thinking on this subject. You may recall that he's a determinist like Dennett (if at times, like him, a rather equivocal one) who rejects mainstream free will and fully accepts the fact that we come into the world trailing clouds, not of glory, but of very variable luck. He knows that we are not in control of this and that we are in no way self-created. So what does he think about moral responsibility? Let me start with a quote [10]:

Many arguments that purport to debunk free will are powerful only if you buy into the often unstated premise that real responsibility is ultimate responsibility. [The philosopher] Saul Smilansky at least has the decency [sic] to make this assumption explicit. In what I take to be the ultimate example of the fixation on the ultimate, he writes, "if there is no libertarian free will, no one can be ultimately in control, ultimately responsible, for [the] self and its determinations. *Everything* that takes place on the compatibilist level ... ultimately deriv[es] from causes beyond the control of the participants." I couldn't agree more, but read it again, removing all the 'ultimates' and the case weakens to the point of collapse.

But what is the case that weakens, and what is the result of its collapse? ("Libertarian" free will, by the way, is what I've been calling mainstream free will, and it seems clear that "ultimate responsibility" is another name for moral responsibility.) Baggini rejects the view of those who "define responsibility as though it must be total and absolute" and, in place of the "ultimate responsibility" thus rejected, he puts what he calls "partial responsibility" [11]. This corresponds to his idea of "partial free will", a concept which, as we've noted in Chapter 3, is not without its difficulties. He then claims that this partial responsibility is enough to justify "ordinary punishment, praise or blame" [12], and "ordinary punishment" includes retributive punishment [13]. So here, surely, is another bit of conjuring. The concept of ultimate responsibility, like that of mainstream free will, is smashed to bits, but this isn't supposed to matter, or to make any real difference, because Baggini's partial responsibility, like his partial free will, is somehow just as potent and comes somehow to just the same thing.

But wait a moment, because Baggini thinks there is one respect, and one only, in which there really is a difference. I mention it not because it affects the argument but because it is so extraordinary. He says [14]:

Eternal damnation ... is a very different thing. If your wickedness is not *entirely* your fault, how could we justify punishment without end? ... Ultimate responsibility is only needed to justify ultimate punishment. However ... ultimate responsibility cannot exist, which is perhaps the most convincing argument against the very possibility of eternal damnation by a benevolent God.

I hardly know what to say. Baggini's assertion is that if mainstream free will *did* exist and *did* generate ultimate responsibility, your wickedness would be "*entirely* your fault", and then we *could* justify "punishment without end ... eternal damnation". Really? *We* could justify it? Speaking for myself, I couldn't begin to justify it under any conceivable circumstances. The whole idea is cruel beyond belief, beyond all imagining. But perhaps we should be grateful for this demonstration that the bible has all along been misrepresenting the nature and intentions of God [15].

Here's one last quote from Baggini [16]:

> [The] condition of 'ultimate responsibility' is defined by Robert Kane as: 'To be ultimately responsible for an action, an agent must be responsible for anything that is a sufficient cause or motive for the action's occurring'. That's a pretty tough condition to meet, and it is certainly not one that we would insist on when using our everyday notion of responsibility.

Here Baggini is saying much the same as Dennett said in his Luther argument, and Bertrand Russell's criticism applies in the same way. Yes indeed, "the condition of ultimate responsibility" is pretty tough to meet — it's impossible to meet — but if there *is* such a thing as moral responsibility, that really is the condition which has to be met for it to exist. It is mere sleight of hand to substitute for it "our everyday notion of responsibility", whatever exactly that may be. In fact Baggini seems conveniently to forget that his kind of responsibility is only partial, just as he seems to forget that his kind of free will is only partial. Certainly there's no suggestion in his book that, because "your wickedness is not *entirely* your fault", the percentage by which it isn't your fault should be quantified, and that society's adverse reactions to your "wickedness" should diminish by that percentage.

In truth, surely, the very concept of partial responsibility, like that of partial free will, is incoherent, just a verbal conceit. Partial responsibility in the sense of *shared* responsibility may well be coherent: if Bill and Ben make an unprovoked attack on Fred, Bill pinioning his arms while Ben punches him in the face, it might perhaps make sense to say that Bill and Ben are each of them partially responsible for Fred's black eye. But that's not what Baggini means. What he is saying is that, even if Ben acts alone and blacks Fred's eye all by himself, Ben is still only partially responsible for doing so. There can be no doubt that, in this scenario, Ben's *actual* responsibility is full and complete, so when Baggini labels his responsibility as "partial" he is talking about his *moral* responsibility. And the reason why Ben doesn't have full moral or ultimate responsibility, as Baggini concedes, is that he had no control over the biological and environmental factors which determined his nature. So where and when and how and why does *any* moral responsibility come into the picture? And if it did, how should we understand the relationship between the part of Ben's nature for which he is responsible and the part for which he isn't – do they mix together to make a whole, like the ingredients of a cake? – and how are their respective contributions to any given act to be assessed? I'm sure Baggini would say that none of this was what he meant, but I doubt whether anyone, even he, could explain what he did mean.

Any reader who has waded unscathed through this chapter may hanker for some kind of summing up. Some philosophers would say that moral responsibility exists because mainstream free will exists, and that this makes the sane wrongdoer *deserving* of our blame, hatred, vengeance and all the rest of it. I don't accept this because I don't for a moment believe that mainstream free will does exist. Others would agree that mainstream free will doesn't exist and that our actions are therefore determined, but would still try to justify the attitudes described above on the ground that they have popular support: that they rest upon a popular conception or notion of ordinary (not "ultimate", not "moral") responsibility. But this surely is an example of the logical fallacy called "begging the question" – a term generally misunderstood nowadays, but one which is properly used to condemn an argument which is circular. This argument *is* circular because it amounts to saying that people are right to have these attitudes because they have them, or that moral responsibility must exist because people assume that it exists, or perhaps that moral responsibility simply doesn't matter because people behave as if it doesn't matter. It's an argument which assumes what it sets out to prove, so it proves nothing.

I have just one other point to make about "moral responsibility": I don't really know what it's supposed to *be*. Philosophers who think that it exists will tell us what gives rise to it, and what they think it gives rise to, but they don't seem to tell us what it actually is. The intrinsic meaning of the term itself seems to slip through their fingers, and the need to provide a free-standing definition of it seems to pass them by. If you were an astronomer asked to say what the sun is, you could explain how it comes to be in the sky, and you could explain the effects of its being there, but this wouldn't tell us what it *is*. If pressed, you could of course go on to tell us what it is because you would know. But if philosophers were pressed to tell us what moral responsibility is, I'm not at all sure that they could because I'm not sure that they do know. And I think this is because, like free will itself, it's a nonsense idea.

9

Vengeance is ours

The interdependence of free will and human savagery

[To punish offenders], or add to their punishment, on the ground that they deserve it because they have somehow failed to make proper use of their free will, is ... well, let's call a spade a spade: it's savagery, cruelty. (NFW, p. 135)

What we were looking for in the previous chapter was some credible way of establishing a moral responsibility – or indeed any kind of responsibility – which would nullify or bypass deterministic luck and make people *deserving* of all the things to which their bad behaviour gives rise under the present dispensation. I cannot see a way of doing this.

But there's another point to be made before we go any further. Just suppose that it really were possible to establish moral responsibility, ultimate responsibility – perhaps by showing somehow or other that mainstream free will isn't the nonsensical idea that I believe it to be and that it exists in some coherent form. Suppose, in fact, that the answer to the "Could he have done otherwise?" question was Yes – yes, he could, and he really might have done. Would this justify the social status quo? Would it justify the moral status quo? Would it justify all the things that people's bad behaviour triggers? Would it, for example, make criminals deserving of retributive punishment? Would it make it *right* to inflict this kind of punishment? I don't see that it would. Wouldn't there be another hurdle to surmount before we could say that it was right? Moral responsibility, ultimate responsibility, mainstream free will ... if these things did exist they would simply add up to a factual state of affairs, an aspect of the human condition. You cannot logically deduce the answer to a moral question from the existence of a factual situation (it's an old and true philosophical proposition that you can't get an "ought" from an "is"), and the justifiability of retribution *is* a moral question. Is it actually *right*, whatever kind of free will or responsibility we might establish, to inflict suffering or enhanced suffering on people to no constructive purpose at all save perhaps to satisfy the desires of other people? Personally I don't have an answer and I don't feel bound to find one because I don't believe in moral responsibility anyway. But there are plenty of people – plenty of philosophers – who do believe in it, and they don't seem to concern themselves with this question. For them the idea of moral responsibility seems of itself, and without the need for any intermediate step or further reasoning, to lead straight to retribution and all the rest of the moral status quo. Very often, indeed, they seem to see "moral responsibility" as a sort of Aladdin's lamp which, if only they can find it, will generate the whole of our existing climate of "morality" without even the need for a quick rub and a plea to the genie. Surely they're wrong. Jesus's injunction to turn the other cheek, though no one acts upon it fully and I'm not recommending it, does at least show that retributive punishment would not be a logical or necessary consequence of our being "morally responsible" for what we do [1].

The fact that philosophers don't seem to ask this question, taken together with the eagerness of many of them to brush their avowed determinism aside in order to validate and build upon our "everyday notion of responsibility", points inevitably to one conclusion: that they, in common with nearly all the rest of us, set a very great deal of store by continuing to live in a society which is characterised by unfairness and which, in some circumstances, sanctions and encourages the deliberate infliction of suffering on other people (and perhaps I should have italicised the word "other"). There's no suggestion anywhere of any qualms about this. Of course there certainly are some determinist philosophers who insist that retributive attitudes are *not* justified – and all honour to them – but those who argue in favour of these attitudes never seem to do so with any reluctance. They are not being driven unwillingly to conclusions they would rather not reach: it is clear, on the contrary, that these conclusions are the ones they want to reach. Dennett is, to put it mildly, eager to uphold the moral status quo, and Baggini embraces retributive punishment happily and without regret.

In so far as this book has been concerned with determinist philosophers who try to uphold free will – compatibilists – this is the point to which earlier chapters have been leading. I've tried to show that these philosophers do it largely for emotional reasons; I've tried to show that it is the inherent ambiguity of the concept itself which allows them to do it; and I've tried to show a little of how they do it. I've tried also to indicate that, in doing it, they draw strength and support from the established and conventional attitudes that prevail among people in general. We may feel confident that if society at large did not nurture the idea of free will and welcome support for it, very few if any of these philosophers would still be saying what they say. So what *is* the emotional component of human nature that, in order to justify and sanction its expression, requires the idea of free will to be kept in place? The answer, I'm going to suggest, is savagery.

Could I propose a thought experiment? Aldous Huxley's *Brave New World* [2] is set in the year 2540. Natural reproduction has ended and human embryos are produced in hatcheries and raised in conditioning centres from which they emerge as five different "castes", the lower ones with their intellects deliberately stunted. Let's imagine a slightly different scenario in which we are joined in our world by a new group of people. These others do not have natural births, upbringings and life experiences like the rest of us but, by means of a scientific process, have been brought suddenly into existence as adults, so constituted as we are constituted at the age of, say, 25. They seem just the same as us; and their characters – their natures, their brains – differ just as ours do, these differences being distributed among them in the same way as ours are distributed amongst us. So now suppose that one of them quickly becomes a serial killer. This wouldn't be unexpected because a few 25 year-olds in the existing population do become serial killers. Inevitably we should recoil from him; and of course we should be right to apprehend him and deal with him in such a way as best to secure public protection and to reform him if possible. (I say more about the treatment of offenders in the next chapter.) But – and this is the crucial question – would we think that he *deserves* retributive punishment, a punishment inflicted simply to make him suffer (or suffer more) because he has made others suffer? Would we not say that he doesn't deserve this kind of punishment because he is merely the creation of scientists, the product of the artificial process which has only recently brought him into being with the brain of a murderer? You'll see by now where this is leading, because surely there is no *relevant* difference between this killer and a killer from our existing population. Both have become killers, not by creating themselves as such, but as the result of a process. In the one case homicidal behaviour is determined by the manipulation of scientists, in the other by that of biological and environmental luck. In neither case did the killer have any control over the determining process. The only difference between the two is that one of them was propelled into existence just before he began to kill, whereas the other has taken 25 years to get to the same place. If you think this difference means that the one doesn't deserve retributive punishment, but the other does, I'd like to know why because it doesn't seem that way to me.

The title of this book asserts that the idea of free will is upheld by a combination of sophistry and savagery. I've tried already to justify my reference to sophistry by giving some examples. So far I've offered no very explicit justification for the reference to savagery, but its time has come. The fact of the matter is that the evolutionary history of humankind has not served to produce a species dedicated to the general welfare of its own members or with any strong inhibitions against killing, harming or exploiting them. Quoting one or two psychoanalytically-oriented psychiatrists, I suggested in *NFW* that human beings are born rather as wild animals, fortunately too feeble initially to do much harm, and reach adulthood after a long and difficult civilising process which may fail spectacularly and which, in so far as it succeeds, does so only by imposing conscientious restraints on a savagery which still exists in latent and probably unconscious form. It sometimes seems to me strange that evolution should not (up to now) have done a better job for us. One might think that a pacific human ancestor who was not aggressive towards his fellows, and did not attract aggression from them, would be better fitted to survive and reproduce than one whose contentious nature put him at risk of early death; but quite clearly this view is wrong. The sad fact is that we, as present day human beings, are at far, far greater risk of harm – physical harm, material harm, emotional harm – from members of our own species than from any other source [3].

You may well resent my suggestion that savagery is a general characteristic of the human race [4]. Look, you may say, at our welfare state. Look at our charitable gifts. Look at government aid to foreign countries. Look, perhaps above all, at the simple acts of kindness which people show to one another every day. Agreed; but I'm not suggesting that we are savage to the exclusion of all else, or that our every action is a savage one: of course not. You may well assert, too, that although there are certainly a lot of bad guys in the world, they are quite different from us because we're not bad guys. And of course it's true that the savagery I'm talking about does show itself in the behaviour of the people we call bad, but really and truly it resides in us as well as in them and one of our outlets for it lies in the way in which we regard and treat them. We're accustomed to draw this distinction between the bad guys and the good guys: the bad guys do the bad things because they're bad and the good guys (that's the rest of us) don't do any really bad things at all. It's an "us and them" distinction and it appears in most societies, although of course some societies change the labels around. At the moment the greatest deliberate savagery on the planet seems to consist in the doings of Isis, and they are at the top of our list of bad guys, but to them – guided as they claim to be by religious imperatives which are alien and incomprehensible to us – we are the bad guys and they are the good ones. And if we had had their biological and environmental luck we should be siding with them.

Nor should we forget that some of the worst things that happen in so-called Islamic State, such as oppressing women, killing homosexuals, and beheading people or burning them to death for religious heresy, happened in our Western world just a few generations ago. In medieval France homosexuals were castrated and, if that didn't work, dismembered and burnt. More recently in England people were boiled or burnt to death, beheaded, or drawn and quartered, often for religious reasons. Paradoxically, women were burned at the stake, rather than being disembowelled and hacked apart, because this was thought more seemly. If they were lucky, gunpowder would be attached to their necks so that when the fire reached that point it would end their suffering by blowing their heads off, but this didn't always happen and it didn't happen to Joan of Arc. In the United Kingdom the last public hanging took place only 150 years ago and the last "private" one as recently as 1964. Capital punishment still persists in many other countries, including America.

In the early nineteen-sixties, Peggy Seeger and Ewan MacColl wrote *The Ballad of Jimmy Wilson*. The last chorus began:

In these more enlightened days,
No room for all these savage ways …

Vengeance is ours

These words were, of course, ironic: Jimmy Wilson was a black janitor who had recently been sentenced to death in Alabama for forcibly stealing the sum of one dollar and ninety-five cents. In mercy, his sentence was reduced to imprisonment for life. And in a review article published as recently as 1998, Dan Kahan, now a Professor not only of Law but of Psychology at Yale Law School, describes with apparent approval the degradation and violence suffered by those held within the American prison system [5]:

> By stripping individuals of liberty – a venerated symbol of individual worth in our culture – and by inflicting countless other indignities – from exposure to the view of others when urinating and defecating to rape at the hands of other inmates – prison unambiguously marks the lowness of those we consign to it.

Quite clearly this regime is as stupid as it is savage, because it must necessarily foster and perpetuate the criminality of those subjected to it. One might think that, as a professor of psychology, Kahan would be impelled to point this out. And his apparent failure to condemn the regime is surely both inhumane and just a little crazy, because it suggests that the rapists, as well as having a better time than the raped, are actually doing quite a good job in furthering the aims of the system. (Is there any point in asking whether, if Kahan himself had had the bad biological and environmental luck to be in jail instead of Yale, he would be saying the same thing – if he could find the time to do so between the pleasures of raping or the pains of being raped?)

We have to recognise that some idea of free will – not necessarily a conscious or an articulate one – must lie behind all this barbarity, behind our image of the bad guys. There's a crucial difference to be noticed here. All of us come across people we dislike, and we dislike them simply because they are what they are: our dislike doesn't depend upon attributing free will to them. But when we think about good guys and bad guys we see the bad guys not just as dislikeable but as *deserving of blame* for being what they are, and perhaps deserving of the most terrible punishments, and this does depend upon the idea that they have free will: this deservedness of blame and suffering depends on a Yes answer to the "Could he have done otherwise?" question. We don't see bad guys simply as rotten products of a rotten process, as problems to be solved or threats to be contained or dangers to be disarmed, but as embodiments of a self-generated wickedness which must necessarily and rightly evoke our vengeance.

I'm conscious that I may still have failed to convince you that we are all complicit in a degree of savagery for which some idea of free will (perhaps an unacknowledged one) serves as a cover or a justification. The trouble is that nearly all of us take for granted the ways of the world in which we live and with which we have always been familiar. Pick up a newspaper – any newspaper which purports to provide some general coverage of world affairs – and in it you'll see examples of man's appalling inhumanity to man, of the terrible physical and mental pain which people inflict on one another. Do we feel much shock or surprise? Do we identify with the suffering involved, imagining just a little of what it must feel like? Probably not – or if we do, it's usually only for a moment. Although we may sigh, we also shrug. And then we turn the page and look at the pictures of self-regarding celebrities or men's and women's fashions, or read a piece about the latest diet or a piece that tells us why diets don't work. The fact that these things nestle side by side with reports of inconceivable suffering, given equal or greater prominence, doesn't surprise or upset us. Does this not tell us something about ourselves? Imagine, if you can, a species akin to human beings but to whom the idea of killing or harming their fellows is quite simply beyond their imagining. To a species like that the savagery which we read about every day would be unthinkable, inconceivable: far from accepting it, members of such a species could simply not encompass it. But that's not us, is it – not by a very long chalk? There's a huge moral gap between a species like that and *homo* so-called *sapiens*. And that gap, surely, is filled with nothing else but savagery. I've no idea whether humankind might turn itself, gradually and in the distant future, into a species of the kind I've described – it would be good to think so – but if it did, the change would be absolutely fundamental.

In well-known experiments in the early 1960s, Stanley Milgram showed that a group of ordinary people, when encouraged by an authority figure in a white coat, were willing to give what they believed to be increasingly severe electric shocks to another group of ordinary people, despite hearing them scream, apparently in great pain, and despite believing that the shocks were becoming so strong as to be lethal. In Philip Zimbardo's 1971 Stanford Prison Experiment, mentally healthy college students were divided into two groups, one playing the role of guards and the other that of prisoners. The experiment was due to last for two weeks but it was stopped after six days because of the sadistic cruelty being practised by the "guards". These experiments are said to show that we behave savagely if "authorised" to do so, but of course this could not happen unless the savagery was already latent within us. (Strangely, on the day that I write these words, my newspaper reports [6] the behaviour of the staff of a profit-making organisation to which government, in its wisdom, has entrusted the care of young offenders. Staff members are said to have punched and slapped their charges and "to have boasted of mistreating [them] ... using a fork to stab one in the leg and making another cry uncontrollably".)

As we've noticed, the two experiments just mentioned were said to show the savagery of which human beings are capable if they believe it to be sanctioned by authority. My suggestion is that the savagery of people in general is sanctioned by the authority of the moral climate in which we live, and that an inarticulate idea of free will is essential to the preservation of that climate. There's a reciprocity here: free will upholds the climate and the climate upholds free will. I don't have to assert that each and every one of us is capable of the savagery shown by the subjects of the Milgram and Zimbardo experiments, though I should probably be right if I did. All you really need to accept is that we live with a fair degree of acquiescence within a certain kind of what we are pleased to call "morality". In January 2016, Saudi Arabia executed 47 people (some by firing squad, some by beheading) among whom was a Shia Muslim cleric. *The Times* [7] ran a leading article headed, "A Death Too Far", in which it raised no objection to the execution of the 46 non-clerical victims and criticised the execution of the cleric only because it was "unnecessary" and would provoke reprisals. This was followed two days later by an opinion piece headed, "Saudi Arabia deserves praise not punishment" and sub-headed, "Execution by sword [not by gun?] is brutal but Riyadh remains our best hope for peace in the Middle East". These two articles were unexceptional and probably unexceptionable, and I'm not even saying that the attitudes they display are "wrong" given our world's prevailing moral climate. But the fact that we accept these attitudes without demur must surely show how far away we are from a species whose members are dedicated to the welfare of one another. All I'm saying is that most of us are savage enough at least to acquiesce in, and to welcome, the infliction of physical or emotional pain or even death on others if, although in reality this is undeserved, it is nonetheless sanctioned by a general belief in free will.

There are other words for retribution: they include reprisal and retaliation, vengeance and revenge. And there are many words which describe the emotions which underlie these things: they include condemnation and hatred, rage and contempt. In our world, none of these words carries any bad overtones: we can express these emotions, and sometimes act them out, without feeling guilty or suffering any general condemnation. Bad people show their badness by hurting other people, but we good people show our goodness by hurting them. And it is largely because of this that the idea of free will persists in the way it does. This is why many philosophers search for ways to validate it, or to propagate some incoherent version of it – and, in the latter case, try to pretend that the unfairness which their version leaves untouched is non-existent or unimportant. This is why they search for what seems to me the meaningless concept of moral responsibility and, thinking they have found it, believe that they have justified the ways we feel and the things we do.

Do not, as the saying goes, get me wrong. I'm not presuming to sit in judgment on the human race. Being, in a modest way, a human being myself, I'm not immune to any of the emotions I have named. I react to many things, initially and instinctively, with condemnation, hatred, rage and contempt, although I then become rather painfully aware that these feelings are really not consistent with my disbelief in free will. To accept the fact that free will does not exist and that determinism does exist, is difficult enough, but to accept the consequences of this, and accordingly to change not just our way of thinking but way of our *feeling,* is to go so far against our existing natures that it may be well nigh impossible – especially since most of us don't want to do it.

Suppose that religious fanatics behead innocent people or burn them to death, as indeed they do, or that a sadistic killer tortures and then murders a child. What could be more natural to us, more normal to us, than to want to see such people suffer for the suffering they have inflicted? And what could be more difficult, especially since (remember Frankfurt?) they probably have no conflicting first- and second-order desires but glory wholeheartedly in their deeds, than to see them not as self-created monsters but rather as the products of a biological and environmental process which, if we ourselves had been subjected it, would have made us the same as them? Here again, of course, there is a reciprocity: it is the savagery of the "bad" people which evokes the savagery of the "good" people, and if all savagery were really to disappear there would be no "bad" people.

Someone who was kind enough to read my *NFW* was kind enough also to send me an approving message about it. It ended with this sentence:

> So, for me the "penny has dropped" and I find it such a relief that I do not have to hate those who have wronged others.

This sentiment seems to me very rare. To see our hatred of bad people as a sort of burden imposed upon us by societal norms, by an outdated moral climate, and to be relieved to cast it off – this is indeed exceptional. If all humanity were to feel like this then perhaps we might have some legitimate claim to humanity.

In practice, the few people who try to oppose human savagery will all too often find it turned upon themselves. They will be dismissed contemptuously as "bleeding hearts" or "do-gooders" or, worse, as "self-appointed do-gooders". These reactions show how anxious most people are to preserve the outlets for their savagery – even if this requires them explicitly to ridicule the wish to do good.

10

They're made to do it over and over

But let's kill them anyway

We really feel the need to see "wickedness" in people and to punish them because of it — and I think we feel this need ... because we want to challenge, purge and destroy the wickedness which they embody and display. The mechanisms involved are exactly the same as those which led us ... to hang and burn witches. (NFW, p. 111)

In the last chapter I suggested that some conception of free will was necessary to sanction and underpin the expression of human savagery. Although I was careful to say that this conception might be unconscious, inarticulate and unacknowledged, I think I may still have overstated the case a little bit. It may be that, in order to see vengeance as justified, people in general don't need actually to harbour *any* conception of free will: they just need *not* to harbour any conception of determinism. The only sense in which most people believe in "free will" is that they live happily within the existing moral climate. If you asked them specifically whether they did believe in it, they would almost certainly give a vaguely affirmative answer, but if you asked whether they believed in determinism their answer would probably be a loud and unequivocal No.

The Cruelty of Free Will

My grand-daughter Eve made a brief appearance in *NFW*, and now my grand-daughter Grace has a walk-on part because she gave me for Christmas a very long book called *1Q84* by Haruki Murakami [1]. Two of the characters are Aomame, a youngish woman, and "the dowager", an older, very rich and very influential one. One day Aomame tells the dowager that her best friend's husband was so violent that he drove her to suicide and that Aomame waited her chance and then killed him undetectably "with a single needle thrust into the back of his neck". The dowager says, "What you did was right", and adds:

> If he had lived he would eventually have done the same thing to other women. Men like that always find victims. They are made to do it over and over. You severed the evil at the root.

To say, "They are made to do it over and over", involves a pretty clear acceptance of determinism, but here the dowager seems to be justifying Aomame's act less as a matter of vengeance than as one of hygiene: the world is a better place without people like that, so get rid of them. The dowager then says that by concidence her own daughter was driven to suicide by the violence of *her* husband. This violence was not unexpected because the dowager "could clearly see that the man had a twisted personality": he "had already been involved in several bad situations, their cause almost certainly deeply rooted". Later the dowager describes men like him as "parasitical men, who can only live by sucking the blood of the weak! These incurable men, with their twisted minds!" This is pretty vehement stuff but, whether she (or Murakami) realises it or not, it still smells strongly of determinism. Did the man in question create his own "twisted personality" (the cause of its twisting "almost certainly deeply rooted"), or was he himself a victim of it? Do men like him freely choose to be "parasitical"? Do they freely twist their own "twisted minds"? The answer to all these questions is surely No, and the idea that such men are "incurable" serves only to add to the deterministic flavour of the brew.

But the dowager soon reveals her true feelings. Although she didn't actually have her daughter's husband killed, she has in some unexplained way "destroyed" what she calls "that contemptible man":

> He goes on living, but he might as well be a corpse. He won't kill himself. He doesn't have the courage to do that. And I won't do him the favour of killing him either. My method is to go on tormenting him mercilessly without letup but without killing him, as though skinning him alive.

The dowager then enlists the help of Aomame in killing other men provided only that each man to be killed "*deserves* no mercy". And she reserves "the right to declare the *justice* of my case in anyone's presence." (The italics are mine.)

These mentions of desert and of justice may serve as a bridge between the last chapter and the next. On the face of it the dowager is a determinist who nonetheless behaves as if she believes in free will and the deservedness of very savage punishment. In reality, of course, she isn't a determinist at all: she hasn't applied her mind to the implications of what she's been saying. She's actually blaming these men for something she describes quite vividly but does not recognise for what it is: their own deterministic bad luck — and it *is* bad luck even if it's much worse luck for their victims. I don't know whether the dowager, if questioned (and you would have to be very brave to question her about this because she might just skin you alive), would say that she believes in free will, but quite clearly she doesn't believe in determinism. Perhaps the idea has never crossed her mind, or perhaps she has simply ignored it because she doesn't want to moderate her vengeance. It is, after all, our vengeful impulses which deflect us from a proper consideration of determinism. But she's a fictional character, so who knows? And who knows whether Murakami himself would endorse her views?

11

Serves that piece of crap right

A penal policy without retribution?

[Penal] measures which people would call "soft" may serve in fact to reduce crime, and measures they would call "hard" may go in fact to increase it. But ... for many people, effectiveness is not really the name of the game: even if the facts were clear to them, they would still demand that governments be "hard" on crime. (NFW, p. 138)

In the last two chapters I've suggested that our unwillingness to see the idea of free will replaced by that of determinism has emotional origins in our innate savagery. It's this attitude of ours which helps the savagery out of its cage and seems to justify its expression in the form, for example, of retributive punishment. You'll have noticed, however, that I myself don't believe that "free will" would really justify any such thing. This is for two reasons – first, free will is a nonsense idea anyway and, second, the infliction of suffering is a matter of morality and can't be justified simply by positing a factual state of affairs. Here's a quote from a paper by the philosopher Saul Smilansky [1] (and "libertarian free will", of course, is what I've been calling mainstream free will):

> [I]f people had robust libertarian free will, and were thus deserving of punishment in the strongest sense ...

This seems like a throwaway line, embodying a proposition too obvious to need a second thought, but surely the word "thus" represents a big leap across a wide river of unreason. This is an example of the way in which some philosophers jump, apparently without a second thought, straight from free will to retribution. Sometimes they use the idea of moral responsibility as a sort of stepping stone, jumping from free will to that and then on from that to retribution, but it comes to the same thing, and it won't do. The problem about mainstream free will, of course, is that it requires a disconnect between people's character and their behaviour: an act done in exercise of free will would be (really by definition) an act not determined by character, and an act not determined by character would not show people for what they really are but would show them to be better or worse than they really are – which is, as I suggested way back in Chapter 1, simply a glimpse of insanity. Nothing could be justified by this piece of lunacy – not moral responsibility, not the deservedness of punishment, not retribution, nothing. And even if mainstream free will were somehow coherent – an idea as difficult for me as the idea that pigs might fly – then, as I argued in Chapter 9, it would still be no more than a factual situation from which the *morality* of "punishment in the strongest sense" could not be deduced[2]. The fact that most people would think it could is testament only to the strength of our desire to punish.

In my *NFW* I spent some time talking about crime and punishment. It seemed to me that this was a subject on which, if we were able to accept the non-existence of free will, we really might begin to revise our views. In 2015 I was asked to take part in a conference on the subject of "Justice without Retribution". Broadly, its purpose was to consider how the criminal justice system might work if the non-existence of free will really did come to be accepted. This experience didn't end too well for me, as it happens, but it did force me to think much harder about the whole subject.

Let me clear out of the way one point before we go any further. In *NFW* [3] I ran through the aims of sentencing set out in section 142 of the Criminal Justice Act 2003. Here I'll clarify and expand on them a little:

> **1. Retributive punishment**. This we must take to mean punishment, distinct from any penalty reasonably imposed for deterrent purposes, which is designed simply to make offenders suffer because they have made others suffer.
> **2. Deterrence**. This has two heads. First, deterrence of the convicted offender from further crime. And second, the general deterrence of others.
> **3. Reform and rehabilitation** of the offender.
> **4. Protection of the public**. This has to do with the confinement of offenders who are dangerous. Incidentally, as I argued in *NFW*, this idea that some offenders are intrinsically "dangerous" (as undoubtedly they are) seems to be founded upon determinism rather than free will.
> **5. Reparation** – that is, the making of reparation to victims.

My position, of course, is that offenders do not *deserve* to be the target of any of these aims. If they act as they do because they are the people they are, and they have not made themselves the people they are, then the idea that they *deserve* to be punished or otherwise taken to task for what they do is not sustainable. But it's equally true that no one deserves to be the victim of crime, and it would be absurd to deny that society must protect itself against criminals. Even though they are not morally responsible, they are *actually* responsible and they must be identified and taken in hand in some way. The only question is, in what way?

Apart from the first one, all of the sentencing aims just mentioned can be justified pragmatically, as being (potentially, at least) for the good of society. The only one that can't be justified on that basis is retribution: hence the title of the conference. For many people, of course, the idea of justice *without* retribution is a contradiction in terms: for them, retributory justice is the only kind of real justice that there is. From where I'm standing, the reverse is true: retributory justice is a contradiction in terms. So we must pause for a while on this idea of "justice". The word is bandied about quite a lot. *Justice* is something that those who are wronged demand, something that criminals must be brought to, something that the police say they strive to obtain for the victims or their families. And indeed *fiat justitia ruat caelum*: justice is something that must be done though the heavens fall. But (if you'll excuse my language) what the hell is it?

Justice seems to have two elements. The first has to do with getting the facts right and bringing home the crime to the person who really committed it and not to someone else. When this aspect of justice goes wrong, the result is a failure or miscarriage of justice. No one is going to defend that. But the other aspect of justice has to do with the kind of acts that amount to crimes and the things that happen to those who commit them. A characteristic of this aspect of justice, unlike the first one, is that it is subject to change and very hard to pin down. Like beauty, it exists in the eye of the beholder. The most appalling cruelties have been, and in many parts of the world still are, committed in the name of justice. In his poem *As I walked out one evening*, W.H. Auden speaks of "the burrows of the Nightmare where Justice naked is". As it happens, Auden himself, as a gay man, was ill-served by the so-called justice which prevailed in his time. I can remember being in court when two gay men were sent to prison for fulfilling their natures in ways which are now perfectly legal and can indeed form the basis of a marriage. And this change of attitude has come about to some extent because we have ceased to regard homosexuality as a self-created aberration. Perhaps in time we might cease to regard any crime, or any other anti-social act, in that way.

The Cruelty of Free Will

The category of "crimes" really is subject to constant change. In my lifetime homosexual conduct has been taken out of it [4], and so have other things – the mere possession of pornography, for example – but the category has also been widened to include, for instance, offences having to do with religious and racial hatred and discrimination. It's true nevertheless that there is at any given moment a defined group of acts currently regarded as so harmful as to be categorised as crimes. How should the perpetrators be treated? It is here that retribution holds sway. There is a general feeling that, although regard should be had to the other aims of sentencing, this one has priority: that's why it heads the list [5]. When criminals are sentenced there is sometimes a protest, from the victims or their relatives or from members of the public, at the "leniency" of the sentence. Whether or not the objection is expressed in this way, the underlying message is: "That's not justice". Someone whose child has been killed by dangerous driving may say of the driver's penalty, "Is that all my daughter's life is worth?"; someone crippled in a violent attack may say that although he must suffer from the injury for the rest of his life, the criminal has escaped with a few years in prison [6]. If I were a victim of crime my first impulse might well be to say the same sort of thing. But how much more "severe" would the sentence have to be before it amounted to "justice"? And aren't the people who take this retributive approach to sentencing really and truly – and, yes, understandably – motivated by something not far away from a wish for an eye for an eye and a tooth for a tooth? One thing at least is clear: what they're not motivated by is a simple wish to reduce crime.

Here I must nail some more colours to the mast and say that, although we can very readily sympathise and even identify with the retributive feelings of those who have suffered harm – perhaps life-changing harm – at the hands of a criminal, it actually makes no *sense* for sentencing policy to be motivated by anything other than a wish to reduce crime. And I have to add that this, besides being the only sensible aim, is the only one that can be justified in the light of determinism. If we don't have free choice, then retribution is out — invalidated, finished, done for. And surely we're not justified in preserving it just to fulfil the wishes of those whom criminals have wronged — wishes, incidentally, which vary in strength from one person to another and which some people do not share at all.

But there's a point to be confronted here. Until quite recently I had taken it for granted that acceptance of determinism would point almost inevitably towards criminals being treated — where possible, and I emphasise that — more constructively and more humanely. But apparently there are those who fear that it would point in the opposite direction. Because we were acquaintances in a past life, I was able to correspond briefly about this with a high judicial authority who made the following comment:

> You are I am sure right to say that English criminal law could accept determinism without falling apart. But you are a little hard on the retributive principle, which does at least have the merit of proportionality. Once the justifications for the criminal justice system become utilitarian, there is little obstacle to locking certain people up forever and throwing away the key.

No doubt we should take these fears seriously, but I find it hard to share them. If you strike retributive punishment out of the list of sentencing purposes, why would this make things worse for the criminal? The aim of the retributory element of punishment is to increase his suffering, not to reduce it; and it is this retributory element which causes us *now* to lock certain people up forever and throw away the key: it was retribution alone that kept Myra Hindley in prison until she died. In a non-retributive system, of course proportionality must remain important. It should depend upon the harmfulness (rather than the "wickedness") of the offence: no one would suggest that someone who steals a few postage stamps should be sentenced on the same basis as a serial killer (though you may recall from Chapter 9 that in 1958 Jimmy Wilson was sentenced on exactly that basis in the State of Alabama for the forcible theft of less than two dollars). And of course the system ought not to become simply "utilitarian". Why would it? Surely we shouldn't start suddenly to see criminals as somehow dehumanised just because we recognised their crimes as being determined. If determinism is true then it is something that we share with them. It is a part of the human condition, always was and always will be.

So the bones – the basic elements – of a non-retributive system of justice could be revealed simply by striking retributive punishment out of the list of sentencing aims and leaving the others in place. But how should the others relate to one another? If we were to discard the idea of free will, then surely priority would have to be given to the "reform and rehabilitation" of the offender (and it may be that "reparation" would have a part to play in that). When the offender is dangerous, "protection of the public" would obviously trump reform and rehabilitation – but only so far as it needs to: a dangerous offender who is incarcerated while he remains a threat is all the more in need of reform and rehabilitation if that can be achieved. More difficult is the question of "deterrence": in order to deter – to deter the offender from future crimes and to deter others from committing crimes – a sentence needs to cause some suffering, and this is more often in conflict with reform than conductive to it.

Deterrence is a hit and miss idea. It doesn't work for criminals who offend in the heat of the moment or without thinking about the consequences of their acts or without expecting to be caught. But we can't just discard it as an aim of sentencing. Let's suppose that all an offender really needs in order to stay away from crime in future is to be given a sense of self-worth, given a training and given a job. Most certainly we should try to provide these things, but that can't be all we do because the result would be that crimes could be committed, not just with impunity, but with advantage. People would queue up to get these things and even commit crimes in order to join the queue. All I can say about this is that we as a society should strive mightily to ensure, so far as possible, that deterrence is not *needed*. The solution, so far as there is one, must lie outside the penal system itself. Early in 2013 *The Times* carried an obituary of Professor Norman Kreitman. He was a psychiatrist and poet who became a philosopher and embraced determinism. One day Bishop Richard Holloway asked him how the lives of damaged young people in Glasgow could be changed. According to the obituary, Kreitman "responded briskly: 'Change the determinants.'" Bishop Holloway's response was not recorded but Kreitman seems to have been a very good man so I hope it was polite, yet here surely is another staggering glimpse of the bleeding obvious. Of *course* you need to change the determinants: you don't have to be a determinist to know that. Tony Blair's promise to be hard on the causes of crime is a promise which sooner or later must be kept. Dysfunctional families need to be identified and helped. And young people who are headed towards crime need something more effective and more constructive than the prospect of deterrent punishment to stop them before they get there. Only by these means can the need for general deterrence be reduced and the way cleared for the genuinely reformative treatment of those offenders who still slip through the net and are amenable to it.

Acceptance of determinism would allow us to solve problems in which the current dispensation – based on free will, moral responsibility and retribution – has landed us. In *NFW* [7] I drew attention to the way in which the supposed need for criminal law to preserve at all costs the idea of free will, whilst at the same time trying to adapt itself to advances in scientific understanding, has led to contortions and distinctions which make no sense. To illustrate this, I looked at the extraordinarily diverse states of mind which courts must now try to recognise and distinguish when someone is charged with murder. Let's have a brief recapitulation. At the top of the list (and I didn't mention this in *NFW*, so I'm making good the omission now) is insanity so gross that the accused is simply "unfit to plead" – unable to plead guilty or not guilty or to take any part in the proceedings. This usually gives rise to a so-called "trial of the facts"[8], in which the court decides whether the accused was actually the killer and, if so, whether he or she should be sent to a secure mental hospital [9]. Down a little way is the lesser psychotic state which amounts to *M'Naghten* insanity [10]. This leads to a verdict of "not guilty" but always to incarceration in a secure mental hospital. Down a bit further is diminished responsibility which justifies a verdict of manslaughter. This is now defined in section 52 of the Coroners and Justice Act 2009 (which says, believe it or not, that an offender may actually be *caused* to kill by *an abnormality of mind* arising from a *recognised mental condition* and still be in the mental state necessary to justify a criminal conviction). Sections 54 and 55 of the Act usher in another state of mind, involving a "loss of self-control", which also justifies a verdict of manslaughter. Down a bit further and we have a lesser degree of mental disorder, relevant only to sentencing, which "lowers [the offender's] degree of culpability".

So by my reckoning the Courts may have to distinguish five different mental states (or six if you count normality, whatever that is) when people are accused of murder. In amongst the relevant statutory provisions, besides this reference to a lowered "degree of culpability", you find references to "impaired responsibility", "impaired ability to form a rational judgment" and "impaired culpability". These artificial and hair-splitting gradations of responsibility or culpability, leading to different degrees of "leniency", show what happens when a system which is dominated by the idea of free will tries to keep pace with a science which depends for its very existence on determinism. And all they do, from where I'm standing, is to make the whole system look more and more ridiculous. This process simply cannot go on. If, for example, an attempt were made – as logically it should be made – to refine the law still further so as to take account of recent findings about the ways in which crime is caused by brain abnormalities, chemical imbalances and faulty genetic endowment, then the whole edifice would fall to bits.

Something which permeates the discussion we've just been having, though it hasn't yet been named, is the legal concept of *mens rea* (guilty mind). You can do an act prohibited by the criminal law (the *actus reus*) and still not commit an actual crime unless you do the act whilst in a certain state of mind (the *mens rea*) [11]. It's because the necessary *mens rea* is lacking that people who are unfit to plead, and people who are *M'Naghten* insane, are technically "not guilty" of murder, although they are normally confined in a secure mental hospital anyway. And it's because the necessary *mens rea* varies from crime to crime that you can be found not guilty of murder but still be guilty of manslaughter. *Mens rea* is a variable and sometimes shrinking concept but one which, supposedly, must always be so framed as to preserve some glimmering of free will. Back in the nineteen-sixties Barbara Wootton (later Baroness Wootton of Abinger) suggested that "*mens rea* has got into the wrong place" [12]. She thought that the concept of legal "responsibility" was amorphous and impossible to pin down; that the purpose of a criminal trial should be simply to establish whether or not the accused did the act in question; and that an assessment of his or her mental state should be left until after the verdict when it could be made comprehensively without regard to the artificiality of statutory distinctions, and would then be crucial in deciding on the best and most constructive sentence to impose. One result, just possibly, would be that the bulk of the prison population would not consist, as it does now, of mentally ill offenders left largely untreated.

These revolutionary ideas didn't go down too well with lawyers and others wedded to the existing rationale of the criminal law. They couldn't get their heads around the idea that someone might (in theory) be convicted of a crime without his or her mental state being considered. The kind of thing they said was: Look, there's a crucial difference of intention between a robber who stabs you in order to relieve you of your wallet and a surgeon who cuts you open in order to relieve you of your malignant tumour, and the law must reflect that: *mens rea* (which of course the surgeon doesn't have) must be preserved because they can't be treated in the same way. But arguments like these are a bit silly. If the law were changed in the way Barbara Wootton suggested, it could and would be so framed that the surgeon wouldn't be charged with any offence. Surgeons, after all, have their patients' consent. And in any case the mental state of surgeons, even if in theory it wouldn't save them from conviction, is such that the court would immediately release them – so in practice they would never be charged at all.

Astute readers of this chapter may have noticed that a criminal trial in which *mens rea* does not play any part is already known to the law. This is the "trial of the facts" which takes place when an accused is, because of gross insanity, unfit to plead. Its purpose is to test the evidence and allow a jury to decide whether or not the accused really did the act in question. Since the accused has already been pronounced grossly insane, the mental element is obviously irrelevant here. There seems no reason why a procedure of this kind should not be applied more generally, as Barbara Wootton suggested. In cases of unfitness to plead, of course, it is impossible for the accused to instruct Counsel, raise alibis, give explanations, or do anything else in his or her own interest. This drawback is unavoidable in such cases, but it would not exist at all in the cases to which the procedure would be extended.

I thought that Barbara Wootton's approach made a lot of sense. And surely it would make even more sense in a system in which free will and retribution played no part. One of its great advantages is that it would bypass a problem which I've already identified, one which has become increasingly difficult and which threatens in the end to bring down the whole of the existing system: the need to present the idea of free will in as many different fractions or percentages as is necessary to accommodate greater and greater understanding of the psychological and biological causes of crime.

Well, there you are. I've finished talking about the elements of a non-retributive system. Of course Barbara Wootton's idea isn't essential to such a system but, whether or not it were adopted, I've no doubt at all that a system of this kind would be more constructive and more humane than the present one and – what matters most of all to most people – that it would also serve to reduce crime, reducing in particular the present high rate of re-offending. At the time of writing, there are indications that the government is moving a little way towards a system of this kind, although not too far and certainly not with any explicit renunciation of the idea of free will.

But just as, in this chapter, I've tried to expand on what I said in *NFW* about a full-blown non-retributory system, I feel the need to expand also on the difficulties of implementing such a system in the real world. One obvious difficulty is that a good and effective system of this kind would cost a lot of money, and governments don't like spending money in this sort of way because there are few votes to be had in doing so. Resources at present are wholly inadequate. To take just one example: merely to address properly the needs of prisoners suffering from learning difficulties would by itself consume the whole of the prison education budget [12]. There's nothing more to be said about this except, perhaps, that it may shade into the other problem which I'm about to mention.

This other problem is in a sense psychological. I've been talking rather glibly about a non-retributive system, but can we really see ourselves being emotionally committed to such a system? Myra Hindley has been mentioned already, and perhaps I may take her again as a useful example. Although most convicted offenders are at risk of re-offending, so that the risk must be reduced (and reduced, as a last resort, by long confinement or by deterrent punishment if there really is no better way), I suspect that Myra Hindley was *not* one of these. My guess is that, once she had been convicted of murder and Ian

Brady had been taken out of her life, she was no continuing threat to anyone. Do we feel – and I emphasise the "feel" – that because of this we could happily let her go free? Of course even a non-retributive system would not require us to do that, because *general* deterrence would demand that something unpleasant should happen to her: we can't have people thinking that they could ever commit murder with impunity. But the fact remains that, under a non-retributive system, her imprisonment would be in a very real sense unfair to her. Can we bring ourselves to feel this? I think it certainly *is* so: luck alone has saved us from being just like her, behaving just as badly as she did, and we wouldn't change places or swap personalities with someone like her for all the tea in China. But to accept this emotionally may still, for many of us, be a bridge too far. And of course the problem isn't confined to Myra Hindley: many criminals commit their crimes in particular or extreme circumstances and present no future danger to the public [14]. There is a real sense in which they should engage our sympathy, but can we *feel* sympathy? I suggested in Chapter 9 that the human species has a long way to go before ordinary members of it could bring themselves to see criminals simply as unlucky products of a faulty process.

In *NFW* [15] I told the story of a 1968 television debate. The motion was that "the purpose of the criminal law is, and ought to be, the punishment of wickedness". It was opposed by Barbara Wootton, who argued that its purpose ought simply to be the prevention of crime, but she lost. The majority of voters saw "wickedness" in offenders and prized retributive punishment above crime prevention. The ultimate retributive punishment is probably the death penalty. Attempts were made to justify it on grounds of deterrence, but it was really an expression of retribution. At the time of the television debate, the death penalty for murder had been suspended in the United Kingdom, but it wasn't finally abolished until a year later. Many people, perhaps the majority, want it to be restored. And it persists in many other parts of the world: in 2015 there were at least

1,634 executions worldwide (and this figure doesn't include those in China, where the number is kept secret) [16]. It is still imposed in some of the states of America, and in 2014 several executions by lethal injection were botched, leaving the offenders variously to gasp, groan, choke, struggle and writhe in apparent agony for periods of between half an hour and two hours. The *Sunday Times* reported some American citizens' comments about one of these events: "What that guy got, he deserved"; "Who cares if he feels pain?"; "Serves that piece of crap right ... hope it was painful for him"; "Cosmic justice, a horrible end to the life of a horrible man"; "Why should we give him a humane death when he didn't give his victim a humane death?". Another comment, explicitly based on free will, was, "Can't feel any mercy ... If you can't handle the punishment, don't do the crime". Did I say something earlier about the idea of free will and moral responsibility being an excuse for savagery?

Reactions of this kind are not universal, but I doubt whether they are all that untypical. And it's a very long journey, along a road not much travelled, from the vision of the criminal which these attitudes display to seeing him instead for what he really is: someone who is built to commit the crime in a world built for him to commit the crime in. And even if the man on the Clapham Omnibus (or in the Greyhound Bus) did come to see the criminal in this way, it might make no difference to his attitudes, because people are governed by their emotions and not by reason. I confess once more that, because I am a human being myself, I quite often catch myself wishing for vengeance. This is a natural reaction: it's a primitive one, but primitive is what most people still are. In 1923 we find T.S. Eliot writing to the *Daily Mail* about Edith Thompson, who had recently been convicted of murder, along with Frederick Bywaters, and sentenced to death. Eliot praised the *Mail* for insisting that she be hanged (as indeed she was) and condemned those who tried to save her from the gallows for their "flaccid sentimentality".

The heading of this chapter – "Serves that piece of crap right" – is

The Cruelty of Free Will

taken from one of the American comments set out above. The other day I was reading a book by Geoffrey Robertson Q.C. called *The Justice Game*[17]. Part of it is devoted to his own efforts to prevent the execution of those convicted of murder in former British colonies. The final court of appeal for such offenders was the Privy Council in London and Robertson explains how the Law Lords who sat on these cases were persuaded over the years to intervene more often so as to stop the executions taking place. I feel enormous admiration for Robertson's work and for his condemnation of the death penalty. But he's no determinist, and towards the end of this part of the book he says:

> I am not opposed to summary execution, in cases of necessity: the gunning down of tyrants, and of armed robbers, hostage-takers and terrorists caught in the act. This is poetic justice, in the simple sense that it serves them right. The mistake is to use the legal system in an attempt to dignify killing by the State.

I'm half-inclined to agree with his first sentence: in the world as it now exists, it really may be necessary in some circumstances simply to kill people, though I'm less certain about Robertson's examples of these circumstances. But of course I part company from him when he says that "it serves them right". This phrase is an interesting one. The idea behind it, I suppose, is that what happens to those who are killed is somehow commensurate with the harm they've done (a difficult idea in itself, because there's simply no correspondence between the two), and it assumes that the answer to the question canvassed at the start of Chapter 9 – as to whether, free will or no free will, this sort of retribution really *is* right – is Yes. The bad guy is being served "right", in the same sense that a waiter might serve him dinner. But it's no good: although this may called "poetic justice", it certainly isn't justice of any other kind.

You may be wondering whether I have tried to recommend a

non-retributive system only to end by pointing out obstacles in its way and so pouring cold water on the whole thing. That hasn't been my intention. It's certainly true that there's a long way still to go. But already there are features of the present system which seem to me clearly deterministic, even if they are not overtly so, and perhaps the best we can do (those of us who want to do it) is to build on these features and make our way incrementally towards a non-retributive system, in the hope that our children or their children or *their* children will wake up one day in the future to find they've got one.

12

A new heart also will I give you, and a new spirit will I put within you

Re-making the criminal

None answer'd this; but after silence spake
A Vessel of a more ungainly Make:
"They sneer at me for leaning all awry;
What! did the Hand then of the Potter shake?"

(The Rubaiyat of Omar Khayyam,
done into English by Edward Fitzgerald,
First Edition, 1859, verse 63)

In the last chapter I suggested that, although the other aims of sentencing certainly can't be ignored, the reform and rehabilitation of the offender should be put at the top of the list and retribution should be removed from it altogether. The system should be geared, not to the punishment of wickedness, but to the prevention of crime, and questions about the "guilt" of offenders should be replaced by questions about their harmfulness. Their mental illness or impairment, if it exists, should be treated simply as one determinant among many: it should no longer require the Court to decide by what percentage it has reduced their "free will" and thus what crime, if any, they are guilty of, but should be treated instead as all-important in deciding

A new heart also will I give you, and a new spirit will I put within you

upon the best sentence to impose. This is what might happen if disbelief in free will allowed us to approach the penal system with rationality.

Although I hope that changes more or less like these will eventually come about, I'm not holding my breath. But I did mention that the government seems at present to be experiencing a modest change of heart (if that's the phrase I'm looking for) and there are one or two encouraging signs. In *NFW* [1] I drew attention to Grendon prison and to the results achieved by its therapeutic regime. I said:

> Under our present system, reform of the offender hardly gets a look-in, and our prisons are full of people with mental illness which goes largely untreated. Official statistics tell us that three-quarters of prisoners have below average I.Q.s, that over two-thirds have one or more mental health disorders, and that nearly one-tenth are psychotic (that's to say, insane).

The regime at Grendon recognises this situation and (for the limited number of offenders who go there) sets out to deal with it. Perhaps this therapeutic approach really will come to be applied more widely. I was encouraged by a recent article in *The Howard Journal of Criminal Justice* [2] headed "Thinking Beyond the Punitive Rationale: Promoting Therapeutic Communities as a Radical Alternative to Prison". It starts: "It is clearly evident that prisons have failed as 'rehabilitative institutions'", and goes on to say that "what we urgently require ... are ... radical alternatives to prison that can reach beyond the punitive rationale and offer us a new way of responding to troubled and troublesome individuals."

I was encouraged also to read a newspaper article [3] about the regime at Whatton, a Nottinghamshire prison for sex offenders. The governor "doesn't believe in evil" and directs all her efforts to the prevention of re-offending. "Paedophiles", says the author of the article, "are loathed now as never before. [The governor] makes them feel better about themselves – because it works." The article goes on to describe the prison rationale:

> [I]f you hate sex offenders, you only make them more dangerous. But if you can find it in your heart to think of them and help them to think of themselves as human beings worthy of a future, then you protect a child.

The fact that the article describes this as "a horrible paradox", rather than a sensible and constructive approach (and one, incidentally, which owes nothing to the nonsense of free will and retribution), gives a clue to the author's own feelings, which she later makes explicit:

> I don't like "kindness" in connection with treatment of child molesters. Like anyone, I have no truck with "soft" options. I want to send them to hell, not group therapy in Nottinghamshire.

And there speaks the true voice of the people – the people who still prize the punishment of "wickedness" above the prevention of crime.

There's a strong case (made stronger still by disbelief in free will) for saying that a very large proportion of those convicted of seriously harmful crimes are suitable for therapeutic regimes of one kind of another – provided that "therapeutic" is given a wide meaning, so as to include education and training. For those whose offences are less harmful, community sentences are at least as effective as prison and should be applied more widely. But now I want to change the subject and look briefly at something rather different.

Up to this point we've been talking about reforming the criminal. But what about *re-forming* the criminal? The heading of this chapter, which comes from the Book of Ezekiel (36:26), is meant to introduce this question. Suppose it were possible, not just to induce offenders

A new heart also will I give you, and a new spirit will I put within you

to change their minds, but actually to *change their minds* – or to change their brains? This isn't far-fetched. Professor Hans Eysenck [4] was an advocate of, among other things, "aversion therapy" which involved offenders being made, through conditioning, to associate vomiting or pain with their criminal or anti-social propensities, in the belief that this would destroy or suppress them. So far as I know, this technique is not used today. In the film *A Clockwork Orange* (based on the book of the same name by Anthony Burgess), the main character is subjected to an extreme form of conditioning, and in the film *One Flew Over the Cuckoo's Nest* (based on Ken Kesey's book of the same name), an understandably rebellious patient is subjected to a surgical lobotomy which (to put it mildly) destroys his rebelliousness.

Few people today would defend any of these techniques, but that's not the end of the story. In his book *The Anatomy of Violence* [5], Adrian Raine identifies physical features of the brain (perhaps developmental rather than innate) which lead predictably to violent crime and even suggests that those who display these features should be locked up, albeit in the most enjoyable conditions possible, in order to protect the public from crimes they have not yet committed. In a paper mentioned in Chapter 11, Saul Smilansky refers to the imposition of such conditions (no, really) as "funishment" rather than punishment. Suppose that one day it were possible actually to modify the features of the brain which Raine identifies: would that be acceptable? Already there are available "interventions", called neurointerventions, which have a direct effect on the brain, though at present their effect is biological rather than surgical. There are medications designed to reduce drug addiction. There are medications designed to reduce the testosterone levels of sex offenders, the use of which is often called chemical castration. Who can doubt that, in the future, other interventions will present themselves?

Anyone kind enough to think that I'm about to suggest a solution to these problems is going to be disappointed, because I haven't got one. On the face of it, it matters a great deal whether or not the biological or surgical intervention is made with the offender's consent. If an offender genuinely wants to give up violence and is genuinely willing to do so through a medical procedure which has been fully explained, there seems to be no problem. There are indeed cases in which criminality has been caused by a brain tumour, and no one (least of all the patient) is likely to object to its surgical removal [6]. But the reality of the consent may sometimes be in question. If the alternative to medical neurointervention is long imprisonment or (please let the thought perish) endless punishment, then the consent may not be very genuine. (Alan Turing, the mathematician whose work at Bletchley Park laid the foundations for computer science, was offered chemical castration as an alternative to imprisonment for homosexual acts, accepted it and killed himself two years later.) And what if the offender doesn't consent at all: should such interventions be imposed by force?

What, you may well ask, has all this got to do with free will? Am I not straying far away from the real subject of this book? Well, not really, because some people suggest that the case for neurointervention – even compulsory neurointervention – is strengthened by the idea of determinism. If determinism is true (they may say) then everything criminals *are* and everything they *do* is simply the result of a complex chain of causation which is out of their control: why not just slip (or force) into that causal chain another link which is equally out of their control – a link in the shape of a neurointervention? It will produce desirable results. It's only like repairing a faulty robot. What's the problem? The idea that belief in determinism leads to this kind of thinking is one reason sometimes given for closing our eyes to the truth of it: more of that in the next chapter.

Speaking personally, I don't like the thought of offenders being forced to accept, or bullied into accepting, neurointerventions, but I'm not sure that I can draw a clear distinction between measures of this kind and the kind of sentences which are already imposed and thought to be acceptable. I'm sure there *is* a difference – and a

A new heart also will I give you, and a new spirit will I put within you

huge one – between, on the one hand, giving offenders a term of imprisonment in the hope that this (combined with any appropriate education, training and therapy) will induce them to change their ways and, on the other, requiring them to be held down, anaesthetised and operated on by a neurosurgeon in order to change their brains. But where exactly does the difference lie? Believers in free will might say that the first scenario, if it succeeds, results in offenders making a "free choice" to live a better life, whereas the second one forces a better life upon them. But this distinction will not commend itself to a determinist: if prison succeeds, it does so through determinism, not free choice and, although forced neurointerventions certainly involve coercion, imprisonment itself is not exactly voluntary. Nor can you really draw the distinction on the basis that a neurosurgical intervention changes the brain and so turns the offender to that extent into a different person, because a successful prison sentence (combined with the things mentioned above) will result in a change in the personality of the offender, and this in itself involves to some degree a change in the brain. There's an interesting question here: how different can people become without losing their identities? It's blindingly obvious that an actual brain *transplant*, should such a thing ever be possible, would be equivalent to replacing one person with another person. That would be patently absurd as well as unacceptable, but where is the line to be drawn?

Some questions don't have clear answers. Each future generation will have to decide which neurointerventions, among those currently on offer, are acceptable and under what conditions. I hope their answers will be: very few and under very strict conditions. But I would add a couple of thoughts. The first is that, contrary to what is sometimes supposed, acceptance of determinism ought not to influence the outcome in any way. Determinism, from where I'm standing, is just an inevitable feature of human existence, and always has been. It doesn't dehumanise us. If we are human, then it is determinism that makes us human. Determinism has *caused* each one of us to be a unique individual and, if we value human life at all, we must value this individuality. The other thing I want to say is that, although I don't believe in free will, I do believe in *autonomy*. I believe that all of us must be allowed, so far as possible, to make our own decisions for ourselves – to express our individuality, determined though it is, in the ways we want to express it, determined though they are. Why? Because once this principle is abandoned, human beings cease to be valuable and become expendable. It's true, of course, that autonomy allows us to get things wrong. That can't be helped. If someone else had run my life for me, it would probably have turned out a great deal better – though it might have turned out even worse – but it wouldn't have been my life. Autonomy certainly allows some criminals to get things very wrong indeed, unless and until we intervene to stop them. But even when we do intervene, we cannot treat them as somehow less than human. Because we all know, don't we, what happens when that happens?

13

Pas devant les enfants

Determinism as a dirty secret

[I]f the human race is to drag itself towards
better things (and no one in their right mind
would doubt that it needs to) a great deal
must surely depend on our ability and willingness
to face reality ... To accept that we must
forever maintain a conspiracy of silence about
some important aspect of our existence would
be demeaning. (NFW, p. 89)

When Abraham Lincoln committed the North to fight the South in the American Civil War (1861-1865), his purpose was to save the union, not to abolish slavery, but he knew it had to go: in April 1864 he wrote, "I am naturally anti-slavery. If slavery is not wrong, nothing is wrong". By the war's end he had partially abolished it and he saw the job completed in 1865 by the 13th Amendment. Yet some seven years before the war began he made a speech at Peoria, Illinois, in which he said:

> Before proceeding, let me say I think I have no prejudice against the Southern people. They are just what we would be in their situation.

These words are not quite a ringing declaration of determinism. You

The Cruelty of Free Will

might think that Lincoln was just one of the many people who endorse determinism without realising it. But you'd be wrong. He was a determinist: no doubt about it. He's one of the so-called "celebrity determinists", the famous figures of the past who made no bones about their rejection of free will and their acceptance of determinism [1].

Another celebrity determinist was the great American trial lawyer, Clarence Darrow. (Spencer Tracy played him in the film *Inherit the Wind*.) One quote from him appears in the opening pages of this book. In his article in the *Nevada Law Journal* [2], Sean Daly gives an except from Darrow's closing argument in the case of Leopold and Loeb, two wealthy and intelligent young men who kidnapped and killed a fourteen-year-old boy, apparently just to see what it felt like. Speaking of one of his clients, Darrow said:

> What had this boy to do with it? He was not his own father; he was not his own mother; he was not his own grandparents. All of this was handed to him. He did not surround himself with governesses and wealth. He did not make himself. Yet he is compelled to pay.

Who are the other celebrity determinists? There's Charles Darwin, there's Sigmund Freud, there's Albert Einstein, there's Thomas Jefferson (who died when Lincoln was seventeen). And (here's an interesting thing) there's Mark Twain, author of *Huckleberry Finn*. There's Friedrich Nietzsche, who said: "The *causa sui* [causing oneself] is the best self-contradiction that has been conceived so far; it is a sort of rape or perversion of logic." There's Voltaire and Bertrand Russell and Baruch Spinoza. Spinoza said:

> The mind is determined to this or that choice by a cause which is also determined by another cause, and this again by another, and so on *ad infinitum*. This doctrine teaches us to hate no one, to despise no one, to mock no one, to be angry with no one, and to envy no one.

Pas devant les enfants

We've a very long way to go before we accept that teaching. And there's Arthur Schopenhauer, who destroyed the idea of free will in one sentence: "You are free to do what you want, but you are not free to want what you want."

I don't mention the celebrity determinists just because they're interesting, or just because they lend support to my own rejection of free will, although they are and they do, but for another reason which will soon appear. There is a group of philosophers who have come to be known as the illusionists. They are not conjurors like the one who did or didn't restore the broken watch in Chapter 3: they are called illusionists because they maintain that it would be disastrous if the general public got to know that free will doesn't exist. It may be an illusion but, according to them, it's a *necessary* illusion. We can't do without it, so the illusion must be preserved. According to Daniel Dennett, it would be a danger "almost too grim to contemplate" if the secret of its non-existence were to leak out [3].

Pre-eminent among the illusionists is Saul Smilansky. He himself doesn't believe in free will, but he thinks it would devastating if other people shared his disbelief. It would destroy their respect for themselves and one another, cause a loss of moral and personal confidence, and have an overall effect so adverse that we simply could not live with it. He says [4]:

> Most people not only believe in actual possibilities and the ability to transcend circumstances, but have distinct and strong beliefs that libertarian free will is a condition for moral responsibility, which is in turn a condition for just reward and punishment.

He adds :

> [T]he difficulties caused by the absence of ultimate-level grounding are likely to be great, generating acute psychological

discomfort for many people and threatening morality – if, that is, we do not have illusion at our disposal.

The phrase "at our disposal" is an interesting one to use, isn't it? Other philosophers take a different view. Thomas Nadelhoffer, for example, says:

> [T]o the extent that folk intuitions and beliefs about the nature of human cognition and moral responsibility are mistaken, philosophers and psychologists ought to do their part to educate the public – especially when their mistaken beliefs arguably fuel … unhealthy emotions and attitudes such as revenge, hatred, intolerance, lack of empathy, etc.

Nadelhoffer thinks that "humanity must get beyond this maladaptive suite of emotions if we are to survive".

If I were forced to pick sides then of course I'd be one hundred per cent. with Nadelhoffer, but I see this kind of blank disagreement as support for my suggestion, in Chapter 2, that what free will philosophers are really doing, for the most part, is to rationalise their own individual (and probably unconscious) intuitions. The very last thing that either of these two can claim, surely, is to have reached their opposite conclusions by applying their powers of rational thought to a set of established facts. They are simply telling us about their own feelings, as they might be telling us that they prefer bacon and egg, or toast and marmalade, for their breakfasts. They are, it seems to me, wholly unqualified to say how the general public would react if the nonsensicality of free will were to leak beyond the groves of academe. I have my own thoughts about this and I'll come to these in a moment, but there's something else I need to say before I do.

Whether illusionists like Smilansky are right or wrong, their approach really is deeply demeaning to the human race. What they are saying is that they know better than we do what we should or

Pas devant les enfants

should not believe and that they alone are the custodians of dangerous knowledge which must, for our own good, always be concealed from us – with the clear implication that we're too stupid to work it out for ourselves. To put it mildly, I don't like this idea. That's why I have headed this chapter in the way I have. It's said that middle class parents, anxious to conceal secrets (probably of a sexual nature) from their young, would warn one another not to speak of them "in front of the children". And they would give the warning in French so that the children would be deprived not only of the secrets but also of the knowledge that they were being deprived. (Would French parents give the warning in English?) Maybe it's right to conceal some truths from children, but most of us aren't children.

I've suggested that philosophers are not, by virtue of their calling, qualified to pontificate about matters which belong, if they belong to anyone, to neuroscientists, psychologists, psychiatrists or psychoanalysts (none of whom may, in their present state of knowledge, be qualified to pontificate about them either). But I suggest also that there is, in the case of this particular dispute, some rather strong evidence to be drawn from real experience in the real world. Here's where I want to re-introduce the celebrity determinists. If Smilansky is right, their determinism should have made them lose respect for themselves and other people, made them lose moral and personal confidence, and made them suffer acute psychological discomfort – to such an extent that they should have found themselves unable to live with it. Did any of this happen? I don't think so. I can't claim extensive knowledge of the lives of all the celebrity determinists – I do know that Nietzsche didn't end up too well, though I don't think his insanity had anything to do with his determinism – but all of them managed to live very remarkably productive and successful lives and none of them seems to have been afflicted by the serious ills that Smilansky predicts.

And evidence from the real world extends well beyond the celebrity determinists. Smilansky's own determinism doesn't seem to have reduced him to the abject state he describes. Nor does the determinism of all the other determinist philosophers, illusionists or not, seem to have had that effect on them. The illusionist case seems thus to depend on philosophers being an elite, throned so far above the rest of us that they do not share our frailties. Presumably the elite must include the celebrity determinists as well, and the neuroscientists who reject free will ... but everyone else belongs to the class of the *hoi polloi* or plebs whose lives will be ruined if they are not protected from the truth. Yet even this scenario lacks plausibility because there are quite a lot of determinists among the plebs. I'm one of them and I know several others. And I seriously doubt whether our lives are one jot the worse morally, psychologically or otherwise, for our disbelief in free will [7].

The real fallacy into which the illusionists fall (and I suppose I'm not qualified to pontificate either, but I do believe I'm right) is to suppose that people's emotional lives are at the mercy of intellectual ideas. In reality, the reverse is largely true. When it comes to giving up belief in free will, Baggini [5] quotes the philosopher Shaun Nichols:

> People just aren't going to change. The normal emotional and moral reactions we have are way deeper than all this theoretical speculation. Hume said basically that no amount of theoretical worrying is going to displace your natural moral sentiments.

I think that's about seventy-five per cent. right. I'd very much like to believe that the truth of determinism would *resonate with* our existing moral sentiments and, over time, incline us to widen our sympathies and behave with more humanity; but it's certainly true that what govern us as human beings, and will always govern us, are human feelings, human drives and human aspirations. An acceptance of determinism isn't going to sweep away the emotional foundations that underpin our lives. I think I'm right in saying that human beings are alone among all the living things on the planet in knowing

Pas devant les enfants

that we are going to die. If we can come to terms with that fact, as we seem to do – Philip Larkin said, "Man's most remarkable talent is for ignoring death" – it really shouldn't be too hard to come to terms with the *fact* of determinism[8]. (After all, we can still ignore its implications if we find them too unpalatable.)

Over the years we, as human beings, have abandoned many beliefs which had real emotional significance for us. We gave up believing in a multiplicity of gods. We gave up believing in witches. We gave up believing that we are so important that our earth must be the centre of the universe, with the sun revolving round it. Most of us gave up believing that the human race was created directly by God, and came to accept evolution and our membership of the family of apes. Most of us have come increasingly to disbelieve in the Devil, and to accept that our "evil" deeds come from us alone and not from his machinations. Very many of us now disbelieve also in God himself and in the everlasting joys of heaven and the everlasting torments of hell. Quite a few of us are coming to see that the "self" is not really what we thought it was. And yet ... here we still are, still living our lives – "living and partly living" at any rate [6] – no less happy than our ancestors and still emotionally involved in the world and in its future. Would this really change if free will were added to the dump of our discarded beliefs?

No one knows how long the human race has still to exist. If we don't kill ourselves off in the meantime, the developing nature of the universe itself will eventually put an end to us, so destroying accidentally an accidental life form. But can it really be true that, for however long we've got (and we may have many millions of years), we can and must deny a truth and continue to live a lie? Professor Bruce Waller has given this book a very kind endorsement. He begins by quoting the view shared by the general public and by many philosophers that "[m]oral responsibility and just deserts promote human dignity". He thinks this view is wrong and so, surely, it is: human dignity is not promoted by clinging to illusions.

14

I'm invited to the investiture

But I don't think I'll go

If we could manage for a moment to detach ourselves from our feelings about free will and determinism, wouldn't determinism seem a pretty unsurprising, natural and ordinary idea, and wouldn't free will seem a very strange one? (NFW, p. 83)

Let's have another bit of French to introduce this chapter: *Revenons à nos moutons!* This injunction, the origins of which seem to lie in a medieval French play in which sheep really did play a part, means literally, "Return to our sheep", but its true message is: "Let's get back to our subject" or, to coin a phrase, back to basics. As we near the end of this book, I have an urge to have another look at the real nature of free will.

I spoke in the last chapter of our acceptance of death. We are creatures of the natural world which we inhabit, and our behaviour is governed by our brains which are themselves the product of natural processes. When we die we become pieces of rotting meat and our brains disintegrate within our skulls – unless we are cremated when they burn away to ash instead. I'm not trying to generate gloom, but that's the way it is, isn't it? That's life for you: that really is *life* for you. And yet our belief in free will allows us to see ourselves as gods standing outside nature, invested with powers untrammelled by nature, powers to transcend our *own* natures.

We invest ourselves – infuse ourselves, imbue ourselves – with these powers, but they exist only in our imaginations, not in the real world. When we do this we are doing something which is very familiar to us in other contexts. We know, if we think about it, that kings and queens are ordinary people: their "royalty" and "majesty" are imaginary qualities with which we invest them. We know that the clergy are ordinary people who remain ordinary despite their investitures: it is we alone who then invest them with the imaginary qualities of "holiness" or "godliness". By the same token, those who commit crimes are ordinary people who are driven by their natures to do the things they do: it is we who invest them with the magical qualities of "evil" or "wickedness". And we know now, as twenty-first century human beings, that witches were ordinary people, and that it was other people – cruel, ignorant people – who invested them with the quality of magical, diabolic malevolence for which they were persecuted, tortured, drowned, burned and hanged. In times still further in the past, every natural phenomenon you can think of was imbued with magic, invested with its own goddess or god. Trees, rivers, mountains, animals were not just the products of nature, but the creations and dwelling places of supernatural beings.

And yet few of us accept that the same process, the process of "investing" people and things with imaginary qualities, is at work when see human beings as possessed of what we call "free will" – a mystical, magical power if ever there was one. Why do we close our eyes to this, and how do we manage to keep them closed? In this book I've tried as best I can to work my way towards some answers to these questions. Part of the difficulty, of course, is what might be called the global applicability of free will – the fact that it is supposed to belong (with just a few exceptions) to absolutely everyone. It's one thing to accept that monarchs and priests and witches and even everyday criminals don't really have the qualities with which we invest them, but to accept that free will is another imaginary quality, one that we all think we have but none of us really has, is ... well, something else.

But since the basics are in our sights once more, let me invent for you the story of the injured woman and the three hikers. Once upon a time there was an injured woman lying beside a remote country path. And three hikers came walking along the same path, one after another. The first one walked straight past her, saying to himself that her plight was no business of his. The second one stopped, but only long enough to steal her handbag and a pearl necklace that she was wearing. The third one crouched down beside her, investigated her injuries, tried to comfort her and called for help on his mobile phone: this one saved her and of course she lived happily ever after. So the three hikers behaved very differently. Why? Because they were different people – differently constituted people, people with different brains. Why? Because they were produced by different processes – different combinations of biological inheritance and environmental influence. Why? Because that's the way it goes: it's the luck of the draw. We're no more responsible (in any sense) for the nature of our brains than we are for the colour of our eyes or the colour of our skins.

In saying this, of course, I've painted a deterministic picture of these three hikers – but it's the only picture on which their differing behaviours can be mapped. How would you map them if your picture were a picture of free will? If they've all got free will, they might all have behaved differently despite being the same people. The third one, so far from being kind to the woman, might have beaten her savagely with his hiking stick. No? If not, why not? There's nothing in "free will" to tell you why not. The fact of the matter is that determinism tells you the things you need to know – the things that free will doesn't tell you, though you may think it does. It is determinism alone that tells you what *kinds of people*

I'm invited to the investiture

these three hikers are, tells you that the first is callous, the second is criminal and the third is kind. And it's determinism alone that tells you how they got to be the way they are and what might be the best way to reform the one who is a criminal. Free will tells you none of this.

For those who want to preserve the illusion of free will Daniel Dennett has provided some very valuable advice: take care not to examine it too closely [1].

15

Was it for this the clay grew tall?

Happy 200,000th birthday, *homo sapiens*

*I hate the world and almost all the people
in it ... even the pacifists who keep saying
human nature is essentially good, in spite
of daily proofs to the contrary. I hate
the human race — I am ashamed to belong
to such a species.* (Bertrand Russell)

No one can really say for how long our own particular species of humanity – *homo sapiens* – has existed, but 200,000 years is apparently a fair estimate. Other human species arose and became extinct before ours, of course, and millions of years have passed since humankind shared an immediate common ancestor with the other apes. Think for a moment about the almost unbelievable immensity of our ancestors' struggle and the almost unbelievable length of time for which it has continued. Think of the hardships they endured, the suffering they underwent (no hospitals, no drugs, and if you live in pain and die in agony that's the way it goes), the setbacks they overcame, the skills and knowledge they acquired and the sheer progress they made. Think of the strength of the driving force, the life force, behind it all. And then set this quite extraordinary process beside what is, at the moment, its crowning achievement: us.

Was it for this clay that grew tall?

In the quote at the start of this chapter, Bertrand Russell said he was ashamed to belong to the human race. Many of us must surely share this sentiment, and the extent to which people do share it is a measure of humanity's hope for the future. The chapter heading itself comes from the poem *Futility* by Wilfred Owen, one of the poets of the First World War. He wrote it after the death of a fellow soldier:

> Move him into the sun –
> Gently, its touch awoke him once.
> At home, whispering of fields unsown.
> Always it woke him, even in France,
> Until this morning and this snow.
> If anything might rouse him now
> The kind old sun will know.
>
> Think how it wakes the seeds, –
> Woke once, the clays of a cold star.
> Are limbs, so dear-achieved, are sides,
> Full-nerved – still warm – too hard to stir?
> Was it for this the clay grew tall?
> – O what made fatuous sunbeams toil
> To break earth's sleep at all?

By the end of the war, Owen himself had been killed. In the last lines of this poem, he was talking, not just about his comrade, but about the human race. Did we really come into existence in order to behave towards one another as we do, killing thousands upon thousands of our fellow human beings, year after year, and searching all the time for more effective ways of doing so? Wouldn't it have been better if the earth had remained a cold and lifeless star?

In a paper published in 1957 [1], the scientist Sir Julian Huxley, Aldous Huxley's brother, described mankind as "the cancer of the planet". He was talking about the dangers of over-population, and the full quote made his meaning clear: "If nothing is done to control this increase, mankind will drown in its own flood, or, if you prefer a different metaphor, man will turn into the cancer of the planet". But people didn't like to be described as cancer. Cancer is something that attacks us – when I was fourteen it killed my father very painfully over a long period, and much later it killed my wife rather less painfully over a shorter one – and they didn't want to have themselves compared to it. I think I'm right in saying that the psychiatrist Anthony Storr described Huxley as "out of touch with the way people feel". I thought this an apt comment at the time but … well, the main message of this book, I suppose, is that the way people feel can often obscure the way things really are.

To my mind at any rate, Huxley's comment conjures up a picture of the planet seen as it might be seen by travellers way out in space, and seen as being gradually eaten away, gradually destroyed, by an invasive organism, an organism which we know to be the human race and which we value because we are a part of it, but which the space travellers might well see as a sort of cancer – an unusual sort of cancer actually, because it would seem to them to consist not merely of a huge collection of cells bent co-operatively upon multiplying, but also of separate groups of cells bent upon attacking one another.

While I was trying to complete this final chapter, I watched a television programme about the brain. It looked at the way in which particular groups of people are happy to unleash death, destruction, torture and suffering on other groups of people who usually pose no threat to them. Nazi genocide is an obvious example. Another is the Bosnian war in which a hundred thousand Bosnian Muslims were slaughtered by Serbians. Then there's the "ethnic cleansing" in Rwanda; and so on and so forth. The neuroscientist presenter was concerned with the *circumstances* in which this happened. He said that it all had to do with "in groups" and "out groups". Subjects were shown pictures of a needle being pushed into a hand, and the

Was it for this clay that grew tall?

hand was variously represented as belonging to a Jew, a Christian, a Muslim, a Hindu, an Atheist and a Scientologist. A brain scanner showed that the subjects reacted with great empathy when the hand belonged to one of a group to which they themselves belonged, but with much less when it didn't. And propaganda plays an important part in reinforcing these attitudes. I'm tempted to describe these findings as giving us another staggering glimpse of the bleeding obvious: they weren't exactly unexpected. But what the neuroscientist didn't concern himself with was the underlying savagery itself – the savagery which is there to be unleashed in this way. Perhaps, like most of us, he just took it for granted, or didn't have anything to say about it. If a big dam breaks and the water bursts out and drowns a village, what everyone wants to know is: how did this happen? Why did the dam break, was there a design flaw, were warning signs ignored? But it was the water behind the dam that did the damage, and no one asks questions about the nature of water. Water is water is water, just as a rose is a rose is a rose, and just as human savagery is … you get the point.

At the present stage of its evolution the human race is trapped by its own savagery. I haven't been arguing, in this book, that our savagery would suddenly disappear if we gave up our belief in free will – sadly, it's too basic for that – but I do think that disbelief in free will would shine a light upon it, let us see it for what it is and encourage us to modify it. I don't want to exaggerate. In recent times, for example, Isis has cut off the heads of its captives, roasted them over fires, drowned them in cages and lowered them into tubs of acid. It has also hooded homosexuals and thrown them from high buildings, sold nine-year-olds into slavery and, on at least one occasion, burned to death a prisoner in a cage to the applause of children. Would they cease to do these things if they could see that their victims differed from them only because a different combination of circumstances had gone into the making of them? Not a hope: they probably couldn't understand this anyway, and why would they try, and why would they care? In 1955 Bertrand Russell joined with Albert Einstein and other scientists in issuing what was known as the *Russell-Einstein Manifesto*. It dwelt on the dangers of nuclear war, asking, "Shall we ... choose death because we cannot forget our quarrels?" and then, in a sentence which was unmistakably Russell: "We appeal as human beings to human beings: remember your humanity and forget the rest." This appeal was entirely reasonable, but of course it made no difference: philosophers do tend to overrate the power of reason.

And yet ... sooner or later, somehow or other, reality will surely catch up with us. And with all due respect to the illusionists (and I emphasise the word "due") I'm convinced that nothing but good will come of it. I hope that some very remote descendant of mine or of yours, making a brief appearance in the world, will find it beset with less savagery and blessed with more understanding because the illusion of free will has finally disappeared. In his poem *Dover Beach*, Matthew Arnold said, "Ah, love, let us be true to one another!" because

> ... we are here as on a darkling plain
> Swept with confused alarms of struggle and flight,
> Where ignorant armies clash by night.

The armies clash not only because they're savage, but also because they're ignorant.

This book has been rather a personal one – too personal for some tastes, I daresay – and I'm going to end on a personal note. The truth about me, as an insignificant member of the human race, is that time gathered me out of non-existence, saddled me with a biology inherited from my parents, saddled me with the changing influences brought to bear on me "in a world I never made" (as A.E. Housman put it [2]), allowed me to live my life as a creature created by a combination of all these things, and then (and probably quite soon now because I was eighty years old last birthday) will spit me out of existence once again. What will have been the point? Well, there won't have been a point: our existence has value only to the extent that we feel it has value.

When my children were small, we took them for a holiday in the Lake District. We had two young girls, and a boy who was even younger. As we walked beside one of the lakes, the conversation turned somehow to the subject of death. My son had yet to come across this idea and my elder daughter thought to enlighten him, explaining about coffins and telling him conversationally that at some future time he would be put into one. He started to cry. The best I could do to comfort him was to tell him that when the time eventually came for him to die he would be quite ready to go, and this semi-falsehood seemed to cheer him up. Some forty years later, tormented by a long period of anxiety and very deep clinical depression, he took his own life. So did my lie prove to be the truth? Not really, because a day or so before he killed himself he told me that he didn't want to die. I took this as a good sign, but it wasn't: it was a bad sign and I should have realised it. Could I have done more to save him? Of course. And does my belief in determinism – my belief that both his death and my failure were determined – make me feel one whit the better? Of course not.

Yet no one has ever complained about being dead. This is not meant as a facetious comment, but rather as a comforting one. I find it comforting. Nearly all of us fear death – if we didn't, the human race would have died out long ago – because it deprives us of all that would otherwise remain of our lives, of all the feelings we would otherwise have felt, of all the experiences we would otherwise have had, of all the hopes that might otherwise have been realised. But after death there exists no entity to feel the deprivation. Then it is only the living who feel deprived. I think that even my son feared death, but for him the world had become a dark place full of unbearable suffering to which he could see no end, and there was only one way out of it[3].

Am I straying again from the subject of this book? Perhaps. But my underlying thought is this. Still driven by the imperative which is inherent in life itself, we continue to live our lives and to procreate so that our children may live theirs, but life is as full of tragedy as it is of joy and there is far, far more than enough suffering inherent in the human condition itself without our adding to it by venting our savagery on our fellow human beings. If this behaviour of ours could be justified at all – and I don't see that it could – then its only justification would lie in the belief that everyone is possessed of what we call free will. And this is just not so. The sleight of hand of the compatibilists cannot make it so. No amount of sophisticated argument can make it so. And the illusionists cannot be allowed to hide the fact that it is not so. When the three wise men in T.S. Eliot's poem *The Journey of the Magi* returned home after going to see the Christ child in the manger, they thought that his birth had changed so much that they were "no longer at ease, here, in the old dispensation". Unlike Eliot himself, I am an atheist: when I die, I don't expect to join my son or my wife, except in the sense that I shall join them both in the state of being dead. And I don't believe that we are all the children of God: I believe that we are all the children of circumstance. But the moral dispensation within which we live embodies as one of its main foundations a belief in free will and in the savagery which it purports to validate, and it is this dispensation that the compatibilists and the sophists and the illusionists want to preserve. It's certainly true that giving up belief in free will would change much of it – but ultimately for the better, not for the worse. In the introductory chapter of my *NFW* [4], I said of determinism:

> I ... think sometimes that most people's wilful blindness to its implications leads to a lot of cruelty and is quite a blot on our civilisation, and that civilisation's next step must involve us in accepting them.

I'd stand by that. Might we not just try taking that next step? Who's afear'd?

Appendix: a summary

I heard the beat of centaur's hoofs over the hard turf
As his dry and passionate talk devoured the afternoon.
"He is a charming man" – "But after all what did he mean?" –
"His pointed ears ... He must be unbalanced." –
"There was something I might have challenged."

(From T.S. Eliot's poem "Mr. Apollinax" about
Bertrand Russell lecturing in America)

There were many moments during the writing of this book when I wondered if I was in full control of my material, putting together my thoughts and developing my argument in a comprehensible and orderly fashion. Or not. So let me see if I can reassure myself by means of a summary:

1. The popular idea of "free will" is the idea that we have free choices – the idea that, in a given situation, we may choose to behave in any one of several different ways. The belief that we have this capacity underlies our justice system and is supposed to validate our retributive responses to the bad behaviour of others. We think that they really could, and really might, have behaved differently and so are *deserving* of blame and punishment.

2. But this idea is destroyed by determinism – a daunting word for a simple and obvious process: that of cause and effect. We are (our brains are) the products of the biological and environmental

The Cruelty of Free Will

luck which has made us the people we are – we're not self-created – and we behave as we do because we *are* the people we are. If our behaviour were not determined in this way, but somehow floated free, then it would shed no light upon our characters and our acts would be inexplicable.

3. So if the idea of free will really is untenable, *how* and *why* does it persist in the way it does?

4. I looked first at the *how*:

> (a) The term "free will" is not self-explanatory, so philosophers can define it in any way they like. Some of them (compatibilists) fully accept determinism but still claim that, merely because we are sane human beings acting without coercion, we have what they call free will. This idea of free will (if it is coherent at all) comes nowhere near the popular conception, because it doesn't even claim to allow us free choice. But most people do not analyse the popular conception and are only too pleased to find some kind of support for their belief that they have something called free will.

> (b) Although belief in real free will is at odds with all our scientific and everyday attempts to *explain* human behaviour, we still manage to preserve it by keeping it tucked safely away in a separate compartment of our minds. There it is immune to these contradictions and can be retrieved whenever we wish to use it for purposes of condemnation. Hypocrisy thus plays a part in preserving free will belief.

> (c) So does sophistry. Philosophical discussion of free will is beset with esoteric arguments, semantics and conceits. In Chapter 5 I give just one example of an argument which

seems to favour the idea of free will but is based upon pure word-play. Many philosophers do seem to find it more fun to play games than to face facts.

5. So what about the *why*?:

(a) In common with many species of philosopher, most people don't want to give up belief in free will because they don't want take on board the changes of attitude which this might entail. Free will belief allows us to go on living comfortably within our society's present social and moral dispensation – a dispensation which seems to me immoral. We can use it to justify both the unfairness of the social status quo (by allowing us to blame those built to fail for failing to rebuild themselves) and the cruelty of the moral status quo (by allowing us to believe that it is both right and just to inflict retributive punishment on those who are built to behave badly).

(b) And why do we want to go on doing these things? Because, it seems to me, the human race is still a savage species which is more than capable of turning its savagery upon its own members, either individually or collectively. This savagery is largely unconscious but it still seeks an outlet, and the idea of "free will" provides one. Although most of the behaviour of most of us is fairly "civilised" for most of the time, our mastery of our innate capacity to do harm is hard-won and fragile and, even if we do not express our harmfulness directly (as very many of us do in very many different ways), we still take satisfaction from its being expressed on our behalf. In our attitude towards criminals, for example, most of us still seem to set the punishment of "wickedness" above the simple prevention of crime – and we do so even though the two aims are usually in conflict.

The Cruelty of Free Will

6. Some philosophers live happily with their own rejection of free will but claim that the rest of us would be incapable of doing so. I think they are wrong. It would certainly be demeaning to the human race if they were right. Surely we cannot go on living this lie until the crack of doom. It would indeed be hard for us to accept the fact of determinism, doing so both intellectually and emotionally, and it couldn't happen overnight. But progress towards real civilisation is always hard – no one promised us a rose garden – and a vast amount of human suffering would be wiped away if we could do it.

Yes, I know there's more in it than that, but a summary is a summary.

Notes

GENERAL NOTE. References in this book to laws and institutions are to those of England and Wales.

Opening pages

1. John A. Farrell, *Clarence Darrow: Attorney for the Damned* (Vintage Books, 2012), p. 38.
2. Bertrand Russell, *Why Men Fight* (first published by The Century Co., 1916).

Preface

1. Richard Oerton, *The Nonsense of Free Will: Facing up to a False Belief* (Matador, 2012).
2. I apologise to anyone who thinks that "status quo" should italicised, but the phrase is used throughout the book and I think italicising it would detract from its commonplace nature.

Chapter 1. Tell me the old, old story

1. Adrian Raine, *The Anatomy of Violence* (Allen Lane, 2013).
2. *The Times*, 7 July 2015.
3. Here and in my Preface and in the rest of this book I treat the brain as the source of our personalities, our characters, our natures, our motivations. A brief explanation may be called for. One of the charms of the *Monty Python* television programmes lay in the characters making lunatic statements with the utmost seriousness, and in one of them a woman looked back with nostalgia on her childhood: "Kids were very

different then. They didn't have their heads filled with all this Cartesian dualism." Cartesian dualism, put forward by the 17th century French philosopher René Descartes, is the belief that mind and brain are in some real sense independent of one another and that, while the brain is a physical object subject to physical laws, the mind is not bound in this way but has some separate existence. Descartes was of course wrong. Whatever the mind *is* – and we won't get into that question here – it owes its very existence to the physical brain. In his book, *Do No Harm: Stories of Life, Death and Brain Surgery* (Phoenix, 2014), pp. 203-205, the neurosurgeon Henry Marsh describes an operation in which he inadvertently tore an artery supplying blood to the brain stem. The patient never woke up and spent the rest of his life a "grey curled-up body" unconscious in a nursing home bed. Marsh draws "the grave lesson of neuroscience – that everything we are depends on the physical integrity of our brains".

Chapter 2. Looking into the abyss

1. Page 83.
2. See, e.g., *The New York Times*:
http://www.nytimes.com/2007/01/02/science/02free.html?pagewanted=print&_r=1&
3. Chapter 7.
4. Tom Burns, *Our Necessary Shadow: the Nature and Meaning of Psychiatry* (Penguin Books, 2014), p. 282.
5. Ernest Jones, *Sigmund Freud: Life and Work* (Hogarth Press, 1957). Ernest Jones's autobiography, cut short by his death, was published as *Free Associations: Memoirs of a Psycho-Analyst* (Hogarth Press, 1959). A passage on page 161 may be worth quoting. It refers to Freud's method of gaining access to unconscious feelings through the patient's free associations (a method reflected in the book's title):

> That apparently disconnected remarks should from the mere fact of their contiguity prove to be bound together by often invisible (i.e. unconscious) links was a brilliant illustration of determinism reigning in the sphere where it was most often denied: it was a most impressive extension of scientific law.

Some would question Jones's use of the word "scientific", but for

Notes

philosophers to do so might evoke thoughts of pots and kettles.

6. It's true also, as Sam Harris has pointed out, that despite the plethora of "rational" arguments which assail them, philosophers seem never to change their minds about free will. Having taken up a position of their own, their primary wish is to defend it against all comers. One reason for this may be that they are unlikely to enhance their reputations as philosophers by confessing themselves to have been wrong. But a more important one, surely, is that they remain emotionally committed to positions which they have taken up for emotional reasons.

Chapter 3. Accept no substitutes

1. Julian Baggini, *Freedom Regained: the Possibility of Free Will* (Granta, 2015). In the remaining notes to this chapter, the references to page numbers are, unless labelled otherwise, to the pages of this book.
2. Pages 193 *et seq.*
3. Page 196.
4. Other names for mainstream free will are "libertarian" and "contra-causal" free will. I shall continue to call it "mainstream" because that's what it is. Evidence (if any is needed) that this really is the free will in which most people believe is provided by a study to which Tom Clark has kindly referred me:
   http://dingo.sbs.arizona.edu/~snichols/Papers/Is_Belief_in_Free_will_a_Cultural_Universal
5. Remarkably, Baggini maintains that our justice system *doesn't* rest on mainstream free will: he says that "the law presupposes no such thing" (p. 150). He gives no authority for this forceful assertion, but he refers earlier (p. 134) to Patricia Churchland, a Canadian-American philosopher, not a lawyer, who "went looking for the concept of free will in the law and legal discussions". It isn't clear whether she went looking in England and Wales or in Canada or in America, but Baggini implies that her findings are relevant to our own law, and certainly all three regimes are likely to agree on this point. He quotes her as saying:

   > "The expression "free will" never appears ... What appears are considerations of *mens rea* [criminal intent] and whether or not there was knowledge of the conditions and so forth. Those are the things that matter, and when there is a dispute about guilt or the proper sentence the question of free will doesn't enter into it."

But if this is true it is only because the presupposition of free will, so far from being absent as Baggini would have us believe, is just too basic, and too deeply embedded, to admit of discussion.

I once drafted a "constitution" for a group of residents bent upon preserving the amenities of our neighbourhood. When my draft came up at the next meeting, one resident expressed something close to outrage because it said nothing about the right to freedom of speech. The constitution was to going operate within a country whose laws recognised this right – up to a point – and a lot of other rights as well, and it was quite unnecessary to spell any of these out (though I confess that I did amend the draft because it seemed to easiest thing to do). If it be the case that the law and lawyers don't say very much about free will, this is for similar reasons: it is something taken for granted and no one concerned with the criminal law would see the need to make it explicit. But if Baggini were to say to one of Her Majesty's Judges who had just imposed a long sentence of imprisonment, "You do realise, don't you, that the offender couldn't have refrained from doing what he did?", he would be told very clearly that the law did not take that view.

It is nonetheless important to reinforce this point. I was directed to an article by Dr. Michele Cotton, *A Foolish Consistency: Keeping Determinism out of the Criminal Law,* which appeared in the *Public Interest Law Journal* (Vol. 15, p. 1), an American publication which Professor Churchland, as an American-based academic, might have considered. I could quote at length from this, but a few early extracts (at pp. 1-2) will give the flavour:

> The criminal law is said to be founded on the idea that persons can be held responsible for their actions because they have freely chosen them, rather than had them determined by forces beyond their control.

A footnote adds that courts and legislatures use the terms free will and determinism "in their most basic sense, as reflecting whether the defendant could have done other than he did." The article goes on:

> The [U.S.] Supreme Court describes as a "universal and persistent" element of our law the "belief in freedom of the human will and a consequent ability and duty of the normal individual to choose between good and evil" ... and has further indicated that the

adoption of "a deterministic view of human conduct" – that is, the view that antecedent causes wholly determine behaviour and therefore that people are incapable of doing other than they did – would be "inconsistent with the underlying precepts of our criminal justice system."

I am grateful to James Miles (whose book is mentioned in the next paragraph of this footnote) for drawing my attention also to an article by Sean Daly in the *Nevada Law Journal* (Vol. 15, p. 992). Daly rejects free will and, in his scholarly and closely-reasoned article, he shows how belief in it has distorted and damaged the American justice system – doing so in ways which apply equally to our own system. I could quote at length from this article, too, but for present purposes a couple of extracts will suffice. The first is from page 1008 (the passages within quote marks being from earlier authorities endorsed by the author):

> The popular conception of free will is "embedded in the very fabric of our system of criminal justice." It can influence the elements of a crime, the defences that can be raised, and the sentence one can receive. The role free will, or "free choice", plays is not subtle either. It is generally recognised that three conditions must be satisfied in order to view an individual as blameworthy, and thus responsible, for his or her conduct: "(1) the actor understood what she was doing; (2) the actor understood that what she was doing was wrong; and (3) the actor could have acted otherwise." Free will is regarded as a central feature ... of the retributive conception of culpability. The legal arithmetic is straightforward. If your conduct was not the product of free will, you cannot be blamed for it. And if you cannot be blamed for your conduct, then you are relieved of responsibility.

In the second extract (from page 1018), Daly quotes the great English jurist William Blackstone (1723-1780) as saying that "punishments are ... only inflicted for abuse of that free will which God has given to man".

Without wanting to make too heavy weather of this, or to hammer Baggini further into the ground (though, really, why not?), I would end with an extract from James B. Miles's book *The Free Will Delusion: How we Settled for the Illusion of Morality* (Matador, 2015):

> Today, the underlying assumption of free choice still exists unchallenged in many corners of the criminal law. English law seems to presume the existence of *liberum arbitrium*, of freedom of

the will – of the idea that people can have chosen to do otherwise. ... [T]he QC Helena Kennedy [Baroness Kennedy of the Shaws] ... [has said]: "I think we'd still hold on to the idea that ... each and every one of us, for the most part, we're able to exercise free will"... Or as Eric Metcalfe, barrister and director of human rights policy at the all-party British law reform organisation JUSTICE put it: "A world in which human beings lacked free will would require a radically different conception of criminal responsibility."

6. *NFW*, Chapter 4.
7. Page 3.
8. Pages 71-72.
9. Pages 72-73.
10. Pages 82-83.
11. *NFW*, pp. 20-22.
12. Page 20.
13. Page 48.
14. Page 52.
15. Page 48.
16. Page 209.
17. Page 56.
18. Page 101.
19. Page 101.
20. Page 131.
21. Page 145.
22. Page 147.
23. Page 5.
24. Page 208.
25. Page 6.
26. Page 81.
27. Page 106.
28. Page 208.
29. Page 211.
30. Page 313.
31. Pages 24-25.
32. Page 140.
33. Page 144, quoting with approval Patricia Churchland.
34. Page 210.
35. Page 91.

Notes

36. Pages 47–48.
37. Page 209.
38. Pages 93–94.
39. Page 96.
40. Page 105.
41. Page 160.
42. Page 209.
43. Page 210.
44. Page 207.
45. Page 96.
46. Page 101.
47. Page 115.
48. Page 168.
49. Page 170, quoting with approval Harry Frankfurt.
50. Pages 164 *et seq*.
51. Page 167. Frankfurt's view leads to conclusions which are absurd, as James Miles's book (see the end of footnote 5 to this chapter) points out (pp. 44–45). Miles makes use of an example put forward by Bruce Waller, on which the following scenario is based. Imagine a fiercely independent African warrior who is captured and enslaved. At first he hates his situation, tries constantly to escape but is constantly caught and severely punished. He is in conflict, wanting to escape, yet fearing the consequences. But eventually he gives up hope, accepts his slavery and identifies with it. Then and only then, under the Frankfurt model, does he acquire the free will which makes him responsible for being a slave. Yeah, right.
52. Page 208, quoting with approval Ken Gemes.
53. Page 145.
54. Pages 146–147.
55. Page 156.
56. Page 209.
57. The biblical story (II Kings 5) would have been more familiar to Kipling's original readers than it is to people today. Naaman was a great Syrian army commander afflicted with leprosy. He went to Israel and saw the prophet Elisha, who told him that his leprosy would disappear if he washed himself seven times in the River Jordan. This was not an obviously medicinal thing to do and Naaman took some persuading, but in the end he did it and of course his leprosy vanished. He thanked Elisha, who adamantly refused payment, and set off back to Syria. But Elisha's servant Gehazi,

The Cruelty of Free Will

seeing the chance to make a fast buck, followed Naaman and caught up with him. Naaman was surprised: "Is everything all right?", he said. "Yes." said Gehazi, "all is well." But then he added: "My master says he knows of two excellent young men who stand in need of money and clothing and if you could see your way…" "Okay." said Naaman, or words to that effect, and he gave Gehazi two talents of silver and two sets of clothes. Being a prophet, Elisha knew what had happened without being told, and when Gahazi came back he said, "Right. Just for that you can have Naaman's leprosy and, what's more, all your descendants will get it too." (Instances of great injustice sanctioned by the bible are not far to seek.) Kipling's poem – perhaps not one of his best – ends:

> Thou mirror of uprightness,
>   What ails thee at thy vows?
> What means the hidden whiteness
>   Of skin between thy brows?
> The boils that shine and burrow,
>   The sores that slough and bleed –
> The leprosy of Naaman
>   On thee and all thy seed?
>   Stand up, stand up, Gehazi,
>   Draw close thy robe and go,
>   Gehazi, Judge in Israel,
>   A leper white as snow!

Chapter 4. What's in a name?

1. Page 185.
2. See the end of footnote 5 to Chapter 3 above. The extract is from p. 41.
3. Pages 42-43.

Chapter 5. A short trip to Frankfurt

1. For the strange consequences of this idea, see footnote 51 to Chapter 3 above.

Chapter 6. Free will and hypocrisy

1. The comment I made in *NFW* appears at the top of this chapter.

Notes

A different but equally striking example of this ambivalence lies in the attitudes of most religious people to disasters or misfortunes of one kind or another. On 4 September 2014 *The Times* reported that, because of DNA evidence, Henry McCollum had been freed from prison in North Carolina, where he had spent decades on death row after convictions for rape and murder. He "hugged his mother and father and thanked God for his release." I wouldn't dream of criticising Henry McCollum for anything he might say in these circumstances and I wouldn't mention his statement at all if it weren't such a typical one. He assumes implicitly that God does intervene in the affairs of the world (something which has sometimes been questioned although, if it were not so, there would seem to be no point in prayer) and thanks him for doing so in order to free him from prison; but it doesn't cross his mind that, by the same token, he might blame God for the original conviction and for the decades spent on death row. Again, on 6 December 2015 *The Sunday Times* reported that when a South African appeal court ruled that the runner Oscar Pistorius, who had been convicted of culpable homicide (or manslaughter) for killing his girlfriend, was guilty of murder instead, the victim's mother said that this was a "success ... due to the justice system and God". She too had no thought of blaming God for the original verdict and she did not think of blaming him for allowing her daughter to be killed.

In order to preserve their faith, religious people must believe that God is responsible for the good things but not for the bad. After the disastrous Indonesian tsunami on Boxing Day 2004, Christian ministers told their flocks to pray for the survivors, but there was no suggestion that a benevolent God might be expected to help the survivors without being asked – or indeed that such a God might have prevented the disaster from happening in the first place. Many other examples could be given of the parallels between ambivalence towards God and ambivalence towards free will but, in the hope that I have made my point, I shall lead this hobby horse back to its stable. (But yes, I do know that the term "hobby horse" doesn't refer to a real horse.)

2. Aldous Huxley, *Brave New World* (first published by Chatto & Windus, 1932).
3. In his book, *The Anatomy of Violence* (see footnote 1 to Chapter 1 above), at pp. 303-305, Adrian Raine recounts the case of a man with no history of deviant behaviour who became a paedophile in his forties. He was found to have a massive brain tumour and, when it was removed, his

paedophilia ceased. A few years later the paedophilia recurred and the tumour was found to have regrown. It was removed again and his behaviour returned to normal once more and was still normal six years later.
4. *The Times*, 28 August 2015.

Chapter 7. If you're not rich, blame yourself

1. Book cited in at the end of footnote 5 to Chapter 1 above. In the remaining footnotes to this chapter, the book is referred to as "Miles".
2. Voltaire (pen name of François-Marie Arouet), *Candide où l'Optimism* (first published in 1759).
3. Book cited in footnote 1 to Chapter 3 above, p. 213. In a book review in the *Literary Review* (June 2015, p. 36), the philosopher Stephen Cave contrasted Baggini's book with that of Miles and made this comment about Baggini's compatibilism:

> But Baggini barely touches on the dangers of blaming people for their lot. In the US, for example, the American Dream – a powerful myth of personal responsibility – results in the poor being held culpable for their poverty … The result is little action to alleviate the causes of poverty, markedly low social mobility and growing inequality.

4. Miles, p. 83.
5. Miles, p. 77.
6. Years ago, in his book *Crime and Personality* (Routledge & Kegan Paul, 1964), Professor H.J. Eysenck claimed that the way in which different people were affected by their environmental experiences varied according to their inborn characteristics (such as extraversion, introversion and neuroticism). Depending on these characteristics, traumatic experiences could lead to crime in some people and to neurosis in others. I conceived a strong dislike for Eysenck, and certainly this approach must be over-simple, but I suspect there was some truth in it. Whether his is still the received view I don't know but neither, I don't mind betting, does Watson.

In 1965, and in very unusual circumstances, I managed to have a Critical Notice about Eysenck's book published in the *British Journal of Medical Psychology*. I started off rather boisterously:

> H.J. Eysenck, professor and populariser, adherent of Pavlov and attacker of Freud, is a controversial figure: to some a knight in shining armour who uses the sword of science to destroy the cant and mysticism of fanciful theory, he is to others a man who for reasons best unknown to himself has chosen to use his declared I.Q. of 180 to put the superficiality back into psychiatry.

At the time I was quite proud of this, and particularly of my reference to "reasons best unknown to himself": it was a sort of in-joke, meant to suggest that he opposed psychoanalysis for unconscious reasons – as probably he did. But before my article was published, an editor or proof reader, thinking there was a typographical error, changed "unknown" to "known". I have never quite got over this.

7. Miles, p. 79.
8. Miles, p. 50.
9. For example, *The Times*, 1 December 2015.
10. Miles, pp. 68-69.
11. Miles, p. 83.
12. In a passage which I can't forbear to quote (pp. 38-39), Miles says:

> When even the world's highest-paid philosophical thinker ... Dan Dennett, defends free will with the comment that we should be "highly motivated to look on the bright side and find the case for free will compelling if we possibly can", and that although "circumstances are ripe for self-deception ... still what one hopes very much to be true may be true" ... we seem to have left academic best practice far behind. Dennett's argument that we should just assume free will and moral responsibility "within limits we take care not to examine too closely" ... and notwithstanding that "any defence of free will against skeptics invites the suspicion of wishful thinking at best, hypocrisy at worst" ... at least suggests that defences of free will may have more to do with species vanity and maintenance of the *status quo* than they have to do with the search for truth or with concepts like justice, equality of opportunity, and fairness.

Chapter 8. Moral responsibility and Martin Luther

1. Quoted in Chapter 4.
2. See James Miles's book, cited at the end of footnote 5 to Chapter 3, p. 91.

3. Nor, of course, does it make sense logically. X cannot do something to Y if X and Y are one and the same.
4. Book cited in footnote 1 to Chapter 3, pp. 154-155.
5. *The Times*, 28 November 2015. The mother's sad self-criticism is that of someone who, although their behaviour is some way back in a causal chain, nonetheless feels responsible for the way it ends. In this case the self-criticism is obviously misplaced: she couldn't possibly have foreseen how the chain would end. In other cases, there may be argument. In November 2015 (*The Times*, 28 November 2015) the politician and ex-London mayor Ken Livingstone suggested that Tony Blair was responsible for the 7/7 bombings which killed 52 Londoners because he was warned that the invasion of Iraq would lead to such consequences. Blair's defenders said this was outrageous because responsibility rested with the bombers alone.
6. It may be sensible to explain the sense in which I use the word "blame" in these chapters because it has two different meanings. A headline in *The Times* for 23 July 2015 said, "Wild armadillos blamed for leprosy outbreak in Florida". Here the word is used merely to suggest that the thing blamed is part of the causal chain which leads to an undesirable outcome: there's no suggestion that the armadillos are morally at fault. (In times gone by there might have been, because animals really were tried and punished for behaviour harmful to humans.) The point would be still more obvious if one were to say (for example) that the weather was to blame for the failure of the crops. But I'm using the word in the *other* sense, the sense in which it really does connote moral fault – and a deservedness of the kind of obloquy which we visit upon those we regard as blameworthy.
7. Dennett's paper, *I Could Not Have Done Otherwise – So What?* is reproduced in Robert Kane (ed.), *Free Will* (Blackwell Publishing, 2002), at p. 83.
8. Pages 93-94.
9. Ernest Gellner, *Words and Things* (Gollancz, 1959). The quote comes from p. 13.
10. Book cited in footnote 1 to Chapter 3 above, p. 77.
11. Same, p. 123.
12. Same, p. 80.
13. Same, pp, 154-155. Baggini's approach to retribution is unusual, to say the least. Alongside the other aims of sentencing, he says that we need

"at least some trace of retribution" in order "get people to recognise the extent to which they can be effective self-regulators". He adds that "forward-looking responsibility is built only on getting people to take responsibility for what they did in the past. To do that, you need some form of retribution ...". Getting criminal offenders to "take responsibility" (or, as I should prefer to put it, to *feel* responsible) for their behaviour is indeed desirable, but to assert that this can be achieved simply by means of "retribution" is surely naïve in the extreme. A therapeutic, rehabilitative approach seems more likely to achieve this aim, if it can be achieved at all. But if retributive punishment really were apt to do the job, then surely there would have to be a change in sentencing practice because it could hardly achieve the desired result unless offenders knew they were receiving it. So a judge would have to tell them that it formed an element of their sentence, perhaps like this: "For purposes of deterrence and public protection, I sentence you to eight years in prison. But the need for retribution makes me raise it to ten, and I am confident that the addition of these two years will induce you to take responsibility and turn you into an effective self-regulator." This idea really is too silly to pursue.
14. Same, pp. 80-81.
15. Verses 41 and 46 of Matthew 25 leave us in no doubt about God's intentions. Those who lack compassion for their fellows are told: "Depart from me, ye cursed, into everlasting fire, prepared for the devil and all his angels." And, so as to ram home the point: "[T]hese shall go away into everlasting punishment; but the righteous into life eternal."
16. Same, p. 76.

Chapter 9. Vengeance is ours

1. The source of Jesus's instruction is Matthew 5: 39 and Luke 6: 29. The subtitle of this chapter is of course a perversion of the well-known passage in Saint Paul's epistle to the Romans (Romans, 12: 19-21):

> Dearly beloved, avenge not yourselves, but rather give place unto wrath: for it is written, Vengeance is mine; I will repay, saith the Lord.
> Therefore if thine enemy hunger, feed him; if he thirst, give him drink: for in doing so thou shalt heap coals of fire on his head.
> Be not overcome of evil, but overcome evil with good.

The Cruelty of Free Will

The idea that vengeance belongs to God alone, and not to human beings, seems a little at variance with the idea that we should act in such a way as to heap coals of fire on our enemy's head, but we ignore it anyway, just as we ignore the similar injunction of Jesus himself. Yet believers do tend to take God at his word and confidently expect him to exact on their behalf the revenge they want to see exacted. If only for the sake of its impact, let me quote the opening of John Milton's poem *On the Late Massacre in Piedmont* (written after some two thousand Waldesians were massacred by the people of Piedmont in 1665 for refusing to become Catholics):

> Avenge, O Lord, thy slaughtered saints, whose bones
> Lie scattered on the Alpine mountains cold …

2. Cited in footnote 2 to Chapter 6 above.
3. The extent and variety of the harm that people do – and do happily – to one another sometimes seems almost infinite. It ranges from acts of war and terrorism, through torture, murder and stoning to death for adultery, through sex slavery and genital mutilation, through bullying and intimidation, through disability hate crime (in a recent study, 66% of disabled people reported aggression, hostility or name-calling), through antisemitism (and no one needs reminding of the suffering which came from that only seventy years ago, but it still persists), through acts of fraud and trickery meant to deprive others of their savings (in the United Kingdom in a single year there were 5 million instances of fraud, £24 million was obtained by phone scams alone and criminal gangs had lists of 160,000 people who had fallen victim to *multiple* scams of one kind or another), through newspaper campaigns to "monster" people disliked by the editor or the proprietor or simply picked at random for vilification, through parents and others who abuse the children in one way or another, through internet "trolls" behaving like spiteful and unthinking infants, through … well, you can add to the list – but don't be too ready to acquit yourself. Is there anyone among us who has not at some time deliberately caused pain to someone else? I really doubt it.
4. Freud accords as much importance to human aggression as he does to sexuality and here's an extract from his *New Introductory Lectures on Psychoanalysis*, written in 1932 (translated by James Strachey, Penguin Books, 1973), pp. 136-137:

> Our hypothesis is that there are two essentially different classes of instincts: the sexual instincts, understood in the widest sense ... and the aggressive instincts, whose aim is destruction. When it is put to you like this, you will scarcely regard it as a novelty. But it is a remarkable thing that this hypothesis is nevertheless felt by many people as an innovation and, indeed, as a most undesirable one which should be got rid of as quickly as possible... Why have we [psychoanalysts] ourselves needed such a long time before we decided to recognise an aggressive instinct? Why did we hesitate to make use ... of facts which were obvious and familiar to everyone? We should probably have met with little resistance if we had wanted to ascribe [such] an instinct ... to animals. But to include it in the human constitution appears sacreligious ... No, man must be naturally good ... If he occasionally shows himself brutal, violent or cruel, these are only passing disturbances of his emotional life ...
>
> Unfortunately what history tells us and what we ourselves have experienced does not speak in this sense but rather justifies a judgement that belief in the 'goodness' of human nature is one of those evil illusions by which mankind expect their lives to be beautified ...

What Freud says about animals is interesting. We are indeed quite happy to have them described as aggressive, and human beings who behave with savagery are often said to be behaving "like animals". But is there any animal that persistently harms members of its own species in the way we harm one another?

5. Dan M. Kahan, *"The Anatomy of Disgust" in Criminal Law*, published in the *Michigan Law Review* (Vol. 96, p. 1621). In his book cited at the end of footnote 5 to Chapter 3 above, at pp. 260-261, James Miles describes Professor Kahan as "a leading exponent of the shaming and degradation of prisoners" and adds that in his review article he "cites without demur another legal theorist's description of criminals as 'scum' and the 'filth' of humanity, and writes of the importance of cruelty within the penal process".

6. *The Times*, 8 January 2016. Because this particular savagery came to light (most of it probably doesn't), action was taken. Members of staff were dismissed or suspended and the police began an investigation.

7. *The Times*, 4 January 2016.

The Cruelty of Free Will

Chapter 10. They're made to do it over and over

1. Haruki Murakami, *1Q84* (Vintage Books, 2012). The references are to pp. 310-316.

Chapter 11. Serves that piece of crap right

1. Gregg D. Caruso (ed.), *Exploring the Illusion of Free Will and Moral Responsibility* (Lexington Books, 2013), p. 112.
2. Smilsanksy will appear again in the next chapter. He himself accepts that mainstream free will doesn't exist, but he doesn't seem to accept that it *couldn't* exist, or that the morality of retribution needs independent justification whether it exists or not.
3. Page 121. As I explained there, section 142 of the 2003 Act actually calls its first category "punishment", not "retributive punishment", but retributive punishment is what it is because any penalties imposed for deterrent or other purposes appear further down in the list. To the framers of the Act, therefore, "punishment" *means* retribution.
4. Long ago, largely through letters and articles in the legal press, I advocated the legalisation of homosexual conduct. No one expressed agreement: very much the reverse. One of my fellow lawyers accused me of *nostalgie de la boue* (literally "a longing for the mud", but usually translated as "a desire for degradation and depravity"). Another accused me of an "apparently complete and total disregard of any recognisable scale of moral values" – to which I did venture to reply that "[o]ne of the moral aims which I and many others would like to pursue is the elimination of unnecessary suffering".
5. In *NFW* I tried to show that retributive punishment really does dominate the list of sentencing aims, particularly in "serious" cases. This was confirmed neatly by a panel of five judges in the Court of Appeal in February 2014. The maximum punishment for murder is a "whole-life sentence". Offenders who receive one of these sentences have about as much chance of getting out of jail alive as they have of winning a Nobel prize. Doubt had arisen as to whether this was compatible with the European Convention on Human Rights, but the Court of Appeal decided happily that it was. The Lord Chief Justice said that "there are crimes so heinous that *just punishment* may require imprisonment for life" and that judges were still entitled to impose "a

Notes

whole-life order as a sentence reflecting *just punishment"*. (The italics, of course, are mine.) Another extract from the *Nevada Law Journal* article of Sean Daly (see footnote 5 to Chapter 3 above: this quote is from page 1014) is apposite here. (Again, the passages within quote marks are from earlier authorities endorsed by the author.)

> [P]hilosophers and legal scholars generally recognise retribution as the dominant theory of punishment, calling it "the leading philosophical justification for the institution of criminal punishment", and "the criminal law's central objective."

Sean Daly's own approach (one after my own heart) appears clearly from another extract (at page 1021):

> The theory of retribution rests on the public's erroneous conception of free will, and perpetuates moral confusion. Furthermore, by instituting retribution as a legitimate punishment, we waste our scientific and legal efforts on creating spurious distinctions in responsibility when we should be evaluating the efficacy of, and enhancing, our other theories of punishment. Thus, as Roscoe Pound wrote in 1922, "in order to deal with crime in an intelligent and practical manner we must give up on the retributive theory."

Amen to that. A similar view was expressed by the great Quaker prison reformer Elizabeth Fry (1780-1845): "Punishment is not for revenge, but to lessen crime and reform the criminal." The powers that be have put her image on our £5 notes but, 170 years later, continue to reject her view.

6. A striking example comes from a case reported in *The Times* for 24 May 2016. A boy of 17 had been killed by another boy aged 16 who has charged with his murder. Two other boys were also charged in connection with the death. Those two were acquitted, and the first one was convicted only of manslaughter. The victim's mother said, "In any other country that would have been life. But just one of them gets manslaughter for murdering my baby." To her the injustice lay not merely in the sentence but in the jury's verdicts and perhaps in the law itself.
7. Pages 122-130.
8. Criminal Procedure (Insanity) Act 1964, as amended. The Law Commission

(where I spent thirteen largely frustrating years) has recommended some changes in the law which governs "unfitness to plead", but none of these would affect the brief mentions in this chapter.

9. "Trial of the facts" was brought to public attention recently by the case of Greville Janner (Lord Janner of Braunstone), who was said to have sexually abused children. Past opportunities to prosecute him having been missed, prosecution was again considered in 2015, but by that time he was suffering from dementia and unfit to plead. Since there was no chance of his offending in the future, and he would not be sent to a secure mental hospital in any case, the Director of Public Prosecutions decided (not unreasonably) that there was no point in having a trial of the facts. Clamour arose and her decision was reversed, but he died before the trial could take place.
10. *M'Naghten* insanity (see also *NFW*, pp. 122-123) is said to exist if "the accused was labouring under such a defect of reason, from disease of the mind, as not to know the nature and quality of the act he was doing; or, if he did know it, that he did not know he was doing what was wrong".
11. Some relatively minor offences created by Act of Parliament do not require *mens rea*: people who do the forbidden act are guilty of the offence whatever their state of mind.
12. The main source of Barbara Wootton's views is her *Crime and the Criminal Law (The Hamlyn Lectures)* (Stevens, 1963).
13. *The Observer*, 22 May 2016.
14. On 10 May 2016, *The Times* reported the case of a man who had pleaded guilty to a murder committed 31 years before. He was identified only because his daughter's DNA had been taken after a minor domestic disturbance and a match was found between that and DNA left at the crime scene. The judge told him, "You will very likely die in prison". He had not been convicted at any time of any other crime.
15. Pages 139-140.
16. *The Times*, 7 April 2016.
17. Geoffrey Robertson, *The Justice Game* (Vintage, 1999), p. 102.

Chapter 12. A new heart also will I give you, and a new spirit put within you

1. Pages 138-139.
2. *The Howard Journal of Criminal Justice* (Wiley Blackwell, September

Notes

2015), p. 397. The authors are David Scott and Helena Gosling.
3. *The Times*, 30 March 2015.
4. Footnote 6 to Chapter 7 above.
5. Footnote 1 to Chapter 1 above.
6. See footnote 3 to Chapter 6 above.

Chapter 13. *Pas devant les enfants*

1. For more about the celebrity determinists see the Naturalism website of Tom Clark:
   http://www.naturalism.org/philosophy/free-will/doubting-free-will-the-argument-from-celebrity-authority
2. Footnote 5 to Chapter 3 above.
3. Quoted in James B. Miles, book cited at the end of footnote 5 to Chapter 3 above, p. 112. Miles draws attention also (p. 207) to the words of John Horgan, former chief writer at *Scientific American*: "Science has made it increasingly clear (to me at least) that free will is an illusion. But – even more so than God – it is a glorious, absolutely necessary, illusion." Am I alone is seeing the idea of a glorious illusion as a bit of a contradiction in terms?
4. This quote, and the one from Nadelhoffer, are taken from the (as yet unpublished) contribution of Gregg D. Caruso to the conference mentioned early in Chapter 11 above. His title was *(Un)just Deserts: The Dark Side of Moral Responsibility*. Unlike some other illusionists, Smilansky does not suggest that the illusion of free will should be actively invented, or actively foisted upon people, only that it should at almost all costs be preserved.
5. Book cited in footnote 1 to Chapter 3 above, p. 139.
6. T.S. Eliot, *Murder in the Cathedral* (the Chorus in Part I). An extract:

> There have been oppression and luxury,
> There have been poverty and licence,
> There has been minor injustice.
> Yet we have gone on living,
> Living and partly living.
> Sometimes the corn has failed us,
> Sometimes the harvest is good,
> One year is a year of rain,
> Another a year of dryness,

> One year the apples are abundant,
> Another year the plums are lacking.
> Yet we have gone on living,
> Living and partly living.

7. Tom Clark has directed me to evidence showing that belief in determinism does not demoralise which appears on the Naturalism website:
http://naturalism.org/applied-naturalism/living-in-the-light-of-naturalism
8. Tom Clark has drawn attention to the discussion on this topic which appears on the Naturalism website:
http://naturalism.org/philosophy/free-will/fully-caused-coming-to-terms-with-determinism

Chapter 14. I'm invited to the investiture

1. See footnote 12 to Chapter 7 above.

Chapter 15. Was it for this the clay grew tall?

1. C.H. Rolph (ed.) *The Human Sum* (William Heinemann, 1957).
2. From A.E. Housman's untitled poem (first line: "The Laws of God, the Laws of Man"):

> I a stranger and afraid
> In a world I never made.

3. One of my reasons for telling this story is that it gives me a chance to say something about depression. Let me begin with an extract from an article in the *Sunday Times* (9 August 2015) about the actor Robin Williams who had killed himself a year before:

> By most accounts, Williams was in the midst of a severe bout of paranoia and depression. Yet that did not make his final act any easier to comprehend.

Depression, of course, is a mental illness (though I think it might more aptly be called an emotional one) and it is the worst mental illness – perhaps the worst illness of any kind – that anyone can suffer from. Those who are afflicted with severe clinical depression don't just feel sad: they are living in a world quite different from ours – a world empty of pleasure and hope and full of torment, anguish, fear and regret, the nearest thing to hell that any of us will ever experience. My son was determined (and I use that word in both senses) to face it bravely, and so he did, but bravery is no match for an illness like this. When he died, he left behind a son of his own, whose mother did not tell him about the manner of his father's death. I thought this decision was defensible because my grandson was too young to understand what depression was. Sadly it seems that most people, however old, are always too young to understand this – a fact of which the *Sunday Times* article provides remarkable and sad confirmation.

4. Page 4.

Remembrance of things past

Those whose task it is to see this book through the press have told me that (because of the exigencies of the printer's profession) there will be some blank pages at the end unless I can think of something to fill them with. The other day I came across an article of mine which appeared in the *Guardian* newspaper way back in 1985. I've no recollection of having written it but it chimes with the theme of this book so I reproduce it here. If it serves no other purpose it will at least reduce the vacant space.

THE GUARDIAN Monday April 8 1985   11

OUT OF COURT

Richard Oerton

IT IS not often that a court belonging to one branch of the judicial system comes into head-on collision with the basic philosophy of the courts of another branch. But it happened in *Meah* v. *McCreamer*, a case decided last summer.

In the light of the full law reports now available, it is possible to see that a judge of the Queen's Bench Division loosed off, not a single shot but two devastating barrels, at principles on which the judges of the criminal courts act every day of their lives. Whether he realised he was doing it is another matter.

Meah v. *McCreamer* was a claim for damages by a car passenger who had been injured by the negligence of the driver. One of the injuries he had received was a head injury, and one of its effects had been to alter his personality. This change of personality was one of the elements of his claim. Nothing at all remarkable so far: the civil courts are full of such cases.

But this particular claimant asked for his damages to be increased because his personality change had taken the form of a change from a law-abiding personality to a criminal personality (or, to be more accurate, from an only mildly criminal personality to a violently criminal one) and as a result he had sexually assaulted two women, raped another, maliciously wounded all three and received a sentence of life imprisonment for it. In other words, he claimed damages because he had been sent to prison.

And he got them. After careful consideration of the medical evidence the judge decided that, but for the head injury, he would not have committed these crimes, so that his imprisonment was simply a consequence of the car accident.

Had the criminal court which sent him to prison for life taken the same view? Of course not. It thought it was imprisoning him because his wickedness required him to be punished, not because he had been involved in a car accident. How else could it think? The criminal justice system exists to identify what it calls "guilt" and to punish those in whom it finds it. The idea which found acceptance with the civil court — the idea that an offender, though sane, may offend simply because of something which has happened to him — can find no place in such a system.

This idea is, of course, scarcely original. Anyone who understands anything of human motivation must accept it and does accept it.

I am not arguing that because Mr. Meah's head injury caused his crimes he should have been let off scot free and allowed to commit some more. The public interest requires that he should be detained in conditions of security; and although one may regret that the detention is taking place in a prison one is forced to admit that his lot might not be much happier (the more is the pity) if he were in a secure mental hospital instead.

No, acceptance of the conclusion reached by the civil court does not require us to make a radical change in the way we treat offenders. What it does require is a radical reappraisal of our reasons for treating them in the way we do, and a radical change in public attitudes.

The logical necessity for such a change is as clear as it is, to many, unacceptable. Immediately after Mr. Meah was awarded his damages, a women's organisation was reported to have said that the award was "utterly disgusting ... like paying the rapist for what he has done."

I said earlier that the civil court had loosed off two barrels. What was the other one? Well, Mr. Meah had been a petty criminal even before his accident, and the civil judge took this into consideration and reduced the award of damages on the ground that Mr. Meah's life of petty crime would have continued even if the accident had not happened and that he would therefore have spent part of his life in prison anyway.

So the judge was saying, in effect, that the remedies prescribed day in and day out by his colleagues in the criminal courts would not have cured Mr. Meah of his petty criminality. But he was also saying something more fundamental: that Mr. Meah was a victim of his own personality before the accident as well as after it. And with him all the other Mr. Meahs.

Can words uttered in the Strand carry as far as the Old Bailey? More important, can they carry as far as Westminster and Whitehall?

Of course the answer to these questions turned out to be No.

Richard Oerton qualified as a solicitor in 1959. He has been book review editor of the *Howard Journal* and has worked in private practice, in legal publishing and at the Law Commission. He ended his professional life as a consultant with a firm of solicitors and parliamentary agents in Westminster. He has produced a number of legal and other articles, written and edited legal textbooks, and written several non-legal books, including this book's predecessor, *The Nonsense of Free Will*.